Recovered, not cured

RICHARD MCLEAN grew up in Dandenong, Victoria and works as a graphic artist at the *Age* newspaper. He is a self-confessed Net junkie and night owl who likes to draw and record music in his spare time. This is his first book.

Recovered, not cured

A JOURNEY THROUGH SCHIZOPHRENIA

Richard McLean

ALLEN&UNWIN

First published in 2003

Allen & Unwin
83 Alexander St
Crows Nest NSW 2065
Australia
Phone: (61 2) 8425 0100
Fax: (61 2) 9906 2218
Email: info@allenandunwin.com
Web: www.allenandunwin.com

National Library of Australia
Cataloguing-in-Publication entry:

McLean, Richard, 1973- .
   Recovered, not cured: a journey through schizophrenia.

   ISBN 1 86508 974 5.

   1. McLean, Richard, 1973– . 2. Schizophrenics – Biography. I. Title.

616.8982092

Designed by Andrew Cunningham – Studio Pazzo
Set in 10 pt Scala by Studio Pazzo
Printed by McPhersons Printing Group

10 9 8 7 6 5 4 3 2

Dedicated to my family, those who endure the chaos, and those for whom the chaos has not yet begun; may they receive love, empathy, and understanding

ACKNOWLEDGEMENTS

There are many people to thank. Notable among them are Mike Bate, Kay Gunn, Mat Vonarx, Jim Pavlidis and Dmetri Kakmi, who stayed with me as the book evolved down the line. At Allen & Unwin, I'm grateful to Erica Wagner for setting me the challenge, and Sarah Brenan for extracting the essence from a raw MS. I thank designer Andrew Cunningham for lightening the load and his talent.

I thank my family and friends, who showed faith in the book's possibilities when I could see none.

I thank Wez with a 'Z', my oldest friend, and all those people – Kirst, Shaggs, Duncan, Captive, Deanne, Ang amongst others – who endured late-night discussions on what is real and what isn't; you know who you are.

To all those people who asked, 'How's the book coming?', thank you too.

To those doctor(s) who diagnosed me and continue to be a support, you're a credit to your profession.

To the authors of the anonymous emails collected offline, I hope you can see the value of my using your messages, and their importance in this book. Heartfelt thanks especially to those who share their concerns and experiences on MSN Schizophrenia Web Community, a wonderful resource and support.

Last but not least, to Karen Conlan, my beautiful friend, without whom this book would not be possible and whose faith in me is incorruptible; thank you.

Contents

Why this book?

This is the story of one person's experience with schizophrenia. I say these days I am recovered, not cured.

I have always liked to draw, even in early childhood. Later I embraced the technology of digital imagery. Some of my digital pictures are included here to open another window on things I was going through, or as reflections on the past. Together they constitute a kind of cumulative visual timeline.

I have also chosen to include messages about schizophrenia from the Internet. These messages, sometimes short, always heartfelt, highlight the uniqueness of each person's experience of mental illness, as well as archetypal themes that are common to carers and sufferers alike. I have changed the writers' names to protect their anonymity.

Mental illness is common, and often devastating. In this day and age it is a treatable condition, yet many are left untreated, misunderstood. I hope that this book will help to demystify it, so that the 10 per cent of people directly or indirectly affected will receive the empathy and care they need.

Richard McLean

CARELESS YOUTH, 1987

*It's midday. We are crossing Dandenong Creek in a working-class
suburb of Melbourne, on our way to the Royal Melbourne Show.
Steve has some mull. We excitedly take tokes from a small pipe
he's hidden in his pocket. We run to get the train – across
a vacant field, up and over the overpass, down the ramp – and
just make it. It's creepy gear, and when the train takes off I feel
I am floating. I can't contain my laughter, life is good.
I remember it as an ideal time. We have a great day; our spirit
is uncrushable. We are young, naive and invincible.*

ANOTHER WORLD, AUGUST 1994

I am crouching in an alleyway. They can't see me here, so for the moment I am safe. There must be hundreds of loudspeakers projecting secret messages, and umpteen video cameras tracking every move I make. My body feels warm, although it is a cold night, and my skin is sensitive to the breeze. The stone wall in front of me is a microcosm of conspiracies: lines, connections, synchronicities. It's also wet, and glints of light on it look like whole universes.

I take a piss. I am nearly finished when a voice says authoritatively, 'Stop that, cunt, or your dad will die of cancer.' I try hard to ignore it. If I respond, they will know I heard it and take the plot to the next step. I must give out that I don't understand, so that the next messages will be more obvious, then I can catch out my persecutors. I have to keep them on their toes, I hate being predicted.

I crouch down near a bin. A cat glares at me, sensing my discordancy. I can see Edinburgh Castle, up in lights for the Festival. They will tie me up, soak my feet in water and have goats lick my feet down to the bone, as described by a tour guide the day before.

Every day I get closer to unravelling the secret plot. Synchronised events suggest the outline of something vast and foreboding, the contents of which I can't fathom. I must find an alias to explore its essence. Whenever a shadowy figure walks past, I think they have the key. Yet I don't intervene, there will be plenty of opportunity when I'm ready to surprise them.

one
Adventures

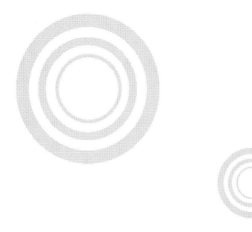

HIGH SCHOOL

I had always liked to study, so even though I'd thought of leaving school all the way from Year 10, I just kept ending up back there. Socially I was always on the periphery but with a finger in every pie. I had acquaintances among the nerds, the Asian group, the Greek group, the wall-ball lads, the cool people, the freaks. I was friendly with some of the teachers too, seeing them as mentors. I was nothing if not adaptable.

I had a lot of friends to hang around with, yet was full of angst. In Biology one day I carved a triangle on the back of my hand with a retractable grey lead pencil. It bled; I wanted it to scar. Bloodletting felt good. Other friends heated up lighters and scarred 'smiley faces' on their arms. Of course I wasn't the only angst-y teenage kid.

To escape from study, we smoked and binge-drank at cheesy suburban nightclubs that I'm sure are still playing 'My Sharona', and 'Blister in the Sun'. I went camping with mates and OD'd on alcohol the night of my deb.

One thing that marked me out as different was my interest in all things metaphysical. Religion was not big in my family, but I was keen to explore the 'big questions' in conversation and through various art forms. All I wanted to do was draw and play music. I thought that would be easy; there were a lot of Arts courses in the VTAC guide. I did not know the difference between 'Arts' and 'Fine Arts'. However, I sussed it out and went for an interview, and I was accepted. I look at drawings from that time, oh so naive. Every creative endeavour seems to reveal its naiveté in time. I'm sure I will cringe at this book soon enough.

ANOTHER BONG: UNI DAYS

I liked university life. I liked the lectures on art, and endless time to draw. I liked the people, I liked getting stoned, and I enjoyed my first few romances.

STREET SCENE
My drawings at this time show no obvious discordancy, but the inclusion of the dog – untouched, and unconnected to the environment around it – is interesting.

I look back at a video from that time. I am with two mates at Kirsten's house. Kirsten is offering me something to drink. I was confused about my feelings towards her; she didn't look like my ideal-looking girlfriend. It was my first inkling that the real and ideal are usually two very different things.

We are all stoned and are recording each other raving about our favourite munchies. I'm a dribbling mess, explaining to the camera the dynamics of 'Vice-Versas'. 'They're like . . . white with black and chocolate with white . . . they sound like this . . .' I move closer to the camera and munch into the lens. Wez is concentrating on recording, you can hear him breathing. The video gets more surreal as time goes on. Another stoned evening.

ECSTATIC

One evening I went over to Kirsten's place. She gave me some orange juice and I accepted gladly. It was the kind I like, with lots of pulp, and tasted refreshing. In the next few minutes I became nervous, and alert. I had the odd feeling of knowing where my body was in relation to the room, and was keenly aware of my weight and the space my body filled. In retrospect I relate it to the exultancy of Ecstasy.

CROSS
A recurring theme throughout my work is flat forms in space, and facades of all kinds. This extends to psychological facades and specifically the role of the media in our society. This cross seems more concrete than the transparent, ghost-like figure in the foreground, suggesting a stronger belief in the artificial than the actual.

I thought Kirsten had put some type of drug in my drink, and I ended up leaving in a hurry, without confronting her with my suspicions. Over the next few years this strange feeling would happen more often. Sometimes food tasted funny, leading me to believe it had been tampered with in some way. I looked for reasons why my body and mind felt so strange. The suspicion I felt at this point was mild, a mere taste of things to come.

MUSIC AND MINORITIES

Jammo was the drummer in my band Bravura. He was lanky and very confident. Jammo said one day, 'Hey, I got us a gig!'

I replied, 'Cool, who's singing for us?', as we had auditioned a few people. The answer was 'You!' It kind of fitted, as I had written most of the songs.

I found I liked performing. Someone had told me that I couldn't do it, and every time I did, I felt good. Even now the best way for me to achieve something is to think of someone telling me I can't.

Life was golden at that time. It was scattered with people to have bongs with. It seemed such a harmless social event, and everyone I knew was into it; no one gave it a second thought.

We would go on trips in my family's Volkswagen to the Grampians and Echuca, burning incense, listening to Janis Joplin, chasing a bohemian lifestyle. We explored each other's minds and celebrated the subversive.

ART AND INVENTIONS

My artwork at this point seemed to have a surreal quality about it. At home I was obsessed with saving the world's energy problem by making an anti-gravity machine out of gyroscopes; I had taken the wheels off Dad's golf buggy.

COKE

My sense of international corporations as vast and untouchable entities will be shared by many; but I also believed they were persecuting me. Perhaps this image hints at bizarre ideas of this kind.
The church is St Paul's Cathedral in Melbourne, and the image is reworked from early sketches.

A dark foreboding sometimes came over me. I would get depressed and have endless conversations with Kirsten. Our conversations danced around the sex issue, yet we didn't ever resolve it. I thought I was in love. I confused that with loving her.

I began to wallow in my biological lows. There was a romantic idea that to be an artist you needed to be a tortured soul in some way. I liked being down.

We did a few more gigs and I had a couple of romances with girls at uni. A few of the guys were a bit of all right as well. For Mind/Body/Spirit week I enthusiastically went to have a session with a tarot reader. I walked away feeling as if I were cursed. Even now I superstitiously avoid reading horoscopes. I guess she exposed, in that brief fifteen minutes, realisations that had yet to surface. As it turned out, the best catalyst was simply time.

DEVELOPING DELUSIONS

I was always pubbing and night-clubbing it with my friends. Once I was at the Espy in St Kilda with the lads. Surveying the crowd, I was thinking about quitting the band. At that same moment, a voice said from behind, 'Hey, there's the guy from Bravura,' but when I turned to see, no one was speaking to me.

I had made a conscious effort to read about what I later understood as 'synchronicity', described by Carl Jung. I was amazed by his interpretation of coincidental meaning, and subscribed to some of his ideas, as I was beginning to

THE SATELLITE PLANT
The plant bears new generations in its root system, while at the same time fertilisation of a terrestrial, human element by a mechanical entity is occurring. I see this image as suggesting at least a predisposition to delusional thinking.

experience the sorts of things he was describing. Meaningful coincidences seemed to happen all the time. I'd be thinking of a song and it would come on the radio; the phone would ring and I knew who it would be. I hid such thoughts from my friends, of course.

ON A TRIP WITHOUT A DESTINATION

I have memories from this time of driving the streets with mates, looking for a suitable 'sticky' bush with which to unblock the bong. Marijuana gave us some good times, and we were as yet unaware of possible dangers.

Always curious to try new things, my mates and I dropped acid one day and caught the train into town. Moo was carrying around a spider that looked like a sea crab. None of us had ever seen anything like it. All my mates had names like Shifty, Skeg, Butch, Doodle; I was plain Richie. The spider stayed with us a long while, being passed from person to person.

COGS

Cities, the media, consumers, all of society is seen as quite mechanical. Facades also figure in this picture: are the cogs on the wall a family portrait or do they exist outside in the landscape?
The opportunity to take some kind of control lies in the remote-controlled car behind the couch.

Each of us marvelled at its form, and the LSD made it more bizarre by the minute.

Butch found a dead duckling in the Exhibition Buildings pond. He acted out a resuscitation, yelling 'CLEAR!' and faking mouth-to-mouth, or should that be mouth-to-beak. Everyone in the park gathered to see what the fuss was about, and people slowed down as they went past, as if to view a car accident. It was funny, yet no one laughed.

Acid became something we would do only occasionally. We faked our way into a gig in the Exhibition Buildings, where people moshed together to the bands, some shirtless, all sweaty, in a plethora of testosterone and pheremones. I can recall an ex-girlfriend saying to me at some such show, 'Look around you . . . can you smell the sex? Everyone here is the product of a fuck.'

We spent the night in the park, talking to two born-again Christian women on their blanket. Watching the now darting stars and lying in the crisp dew, I found my body was cold, yet the air threw warm licks around my arms and hands. Early that morning at about 6 a.m., while our trips were coming down, Moo yelled, '*He's back!*': the spider had returned – but only on acid.

Looking back, I am amazed by the similarities between hallucinogens and psychosis. Indeed, it was a practice in the 1960s to treat the mentally ill with LSD in some circumstances; it was believed the drug could help the process of psychotherapy by liberating subconscious thoughts.

I now know that drugs like marijuana, speed, cocaine, heroin and LSD can cause a brain reaction that resembles schizophrenia. Usually, these 'drug-induced psychoses' will last only for as long as the drug is in the system. However, the taking of such drugs can uncover a mental illness that is latent in the person, or make symptoms worse if an illness already exists. All these drugs increase the production of dopamine in the brain, as do alcohol, tobacco and coffee. It is thought that schizophrenia is caused in part by an excess of dopamine.

Use and abuse of drugs is referred to as 'self-medicating', because the person is usually using the drugs to feel better, or to explain away their surreal experiences.

I am not against drug use, but I do believe in safe drug-taking, which presupposes education about possible risks. Drug use is a personal choice, up to the individual. I have a problem with the decriminalisation of marijuana, however, because it suggests the drug is harmless. I am sure many people know that marijuana can be extremely detrimental to one's passion for life, as well as contributing to mental illness. Recent studies suggest prolonged use can actually cause schizophrenia.

> My son . . . said he wasn't having hallucinations but I would find him alone and giggling about something that was going on in his head. The past week he has become more irritable, sleeping a lot. He has no appetite, stays in, and doesn't see any of his friends. My son has a history of drug abuse prior to his diagnosis. Mostly hallucinogens, LSD etc. He quit using pot because he would trip like he was on LSD and it was too much for him. Anyone out there have any insight or personal experience that might shed some light on this for me?

THE BLEAK AND BITTERSWEET COLOUR OF SAND

I was sensitive to colour, and often had strange visual perceptions. Faces emerged from concrete, little white spots buzzed

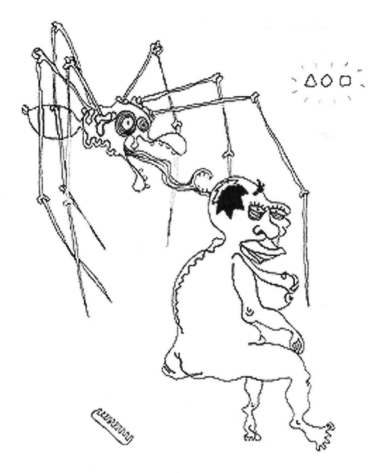

FEEDING

Whenever I had a pen handy, I would draw surreal
little sketches such as this, suggesting the chaos
that would soon begin to envelop me. My ability to
express things in words was limited. Drawing
images crystallised ideas for me, brought them
into the conscious arena.

around when I looked up into the sky. I felt (and still feel) an affinity with neutral tones. Sand colour sits well with me, its softness, harshness and neutral feel, against its state of constant flux. Such thoughts were with me constantly. Dashes of surreal-ness began to enter my everyday life. A leaf, a dead cicada seemed to me to harbour magical qualities, and would set me thinking about life cycles, nature, all things metaphysical.

Architecture too, seemed to take on magical qualities as I traversed old Melbourne town. I thought I could grasp the essence of images seen in galleries, and I saw epiphanies everywhere. In retrospect, all my apparently lucid perceptions were opaque to everyone but myself.

STATION
One positive experience for me, and one that I still have, is that scenes, and especially architecture, can have heightened meaning. Here is a reworked version of a sketch which I tried to render with this magical or hallucinogenic flavour, in the proportion and perspective. In the colour version, the faces are done in a colour suggesting a melting pot of all the world's races.

I continued the social rituals of marijuana smoking, even though the thrill of it had faded. Sometimes bongs made me paranoid – I felt people were picking on me. On the plus side,

I would consume music as if I were absorbing its essence. Marijuana seemed to take me to the purest form of anything I listened to.

Walking down the street I would add together snippets of conversation gathered from people I passed. I had been exposed to the Surrealists, and they caused a paradigm shift in

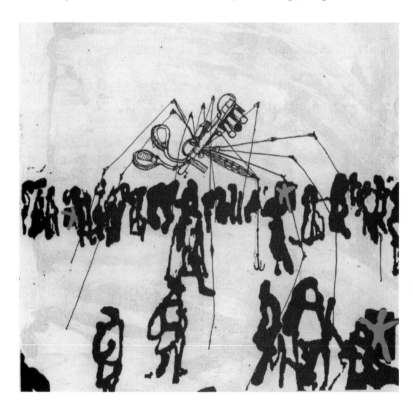

WHEN TECHNOLOGY THINKS
I spent a lot of time around the city, drawing. When I had exhausted obvious points of interest, I'd sketch Walk/Don't Walk signs, street poles and lights. In this image, technology is 'hooking' certain people out of bustling crowds. I felt that I was one whom these magical messages were touching.

my perception of the world around me. Sometimes I perceived what seemed to be magical messages meant only for me, for example, in a comic strip. I would always read the public notices in the *Herald-Sun* for evidence of Dadaist messages.

I became moody sometimes, although I seemed to lack the capacity to express my feelings. I was often depressed, and wallowed in my depression. Yet I was still very socially active. I chatted of all things metaphysical. People used to think I was eccentric, and I liked weirdness, I encouraged it in my life. My perceptions at this time started to solidify into something foreboding.

 I have one question, Is it always this hard in the early days of the illness? Everyone on this website or the majority seem to have lived with it for a fair while I want to know what it was like when it first started for everyone. I want to know that I'm not abnormal.

CHANGE OF SCENERY

'I'm leaving the band,' I told Jammo.

'What are you going to do?'

'I don't know,' I replied. That answer could have been applied to various things.

Uni finished, and I did quite well.

I moved up to Surfers Paradise for a while, as I had a couple of mates up there. At one count, sixteen people were living in the house, all guys. The youthful blokeyness of the joint challenged me as someone not 'out' as bisexual. I knew I liked girls, I knew I liked guys. Bisexuality was something I had never talked about in detail, except symbolically with Kirsten. This was definitely not the place to bring it up.

The house was on Wheelan Street. We used to call it

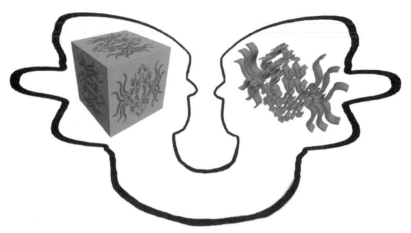

LUST AND DELUSION
In this image, genitalia are rendered symbolically, as one is an
extruded form, the other as a series of facades on the sides of a box.
The box combines alternative versions of sexuality, in line with my
lack of openness about bisexuality at the time. I was not a fan of
black and white, I saw crippling shades of grey in every issue.

'Wheelin' and Dealin' Street'. With sixteen guys living there,
just about all smokers, the dealers would come to our place in
the morning and sell us g's. You would wake up on the
lounge-room floor with a packed bong in your face.

LOSING BRAIN CELLS

I celebrated my eccentricity and spent a lot of time in a local
park, playing guitar and singing. Sometimes we ate our food
at the Salvation Army, which I felt guilty about as I still had a
few hundred dollars left of my savings. The other guys were
on the dole.

We drank copious amounts of cask wine, 'Goonie juice', and some of the guys swindled other people's drinks in nightclubs when their backs were turned. We stuck together, even storming a house with baseball bats in the next suburb to get back some stolen goods we'd had a tip-off about. I just went for the ride. There was conflict for the leadership of the pack all the time. I stayed on the outer, as I always had done. One mate said to me, 'You're the trippiest bloke I know'; I was not aware at the time that it could have been a back-handed compliment.

HIERARCHY
This picture indicates my feelings about hierarchy, especially in connection with money. It celebrates the humble people or underdogs (held in place by the intermediate poles making witches' hats, shown coming out of a box), who have the insight.

INVISIBLE

One night I had some bongs with the guys, and sat perched on the peeling laminate on the kitchen bench, listening keenly to the conversations. I was frozen, not speaking for long periods yet concentrating on the dynamics of what was said and to whom, the hierarchies and the jokes. I had become invisible, frozen in passivity, and expressing none of my views.

SEX

A good-looking guy began to hang out at the house. He was a jokester and very confident and always had his shirt off – he oozed sex. It was interesting how the guys warmed to him. His antics were entertaining, and he was well received in the house. The subversive sexual content of his relations with the guys fascinated me.

Porn mags were passed around and there was a general outburst of 'Looka the tits on that' and 'Fucking nice bit of pouch'. At the time, it seemed to me they were trying to prove to each other how hetero they were.

One night I was in my familiar position on the bench, listening to the two people left. Everyone else had crashed out. Looking back, time just seemed to flick past in an instant. The conversation seemed to resonate with things I was thinking, and yet there were moments when I found it hard to concentrate. Every second it was as though I had just walked into the room; every sentence that was spoken harboured new elements. I was like a goldfish, constantly surprised by the same rock.

I must have looked really freaky, staring at people in conversation for hours on end, moving my head as if I was watching a tennis match, silent and invisible. Was this the catatonic state characteristic of schizophrenia, or was I just really stoned? Things were said that resonated with things that had happened to me days earlier, as if my memory was available to their minds. This is called 'thought transference', and it is a defining symptom of schizophrenia. I was awed at the lucidity of what was being played out before me.

No one I knew, much less me, understood anything about mental illness, and we were not exactly taking care of ourselves. Looking back, I see it was fairly hedonistic.

HOMOPHOBIA

Homophobia was at a generally expected level for a house of straight blokes, and subtle jokes often crept into the conversation. Other times it was more obvious. On the wall out the back was scrawled 'Butch likes it up the arse'. To my jaded and often suspicious mind, it seemed that I was a mere pawn in the hierarchy and all weapons were turned on me. The innuendo I perceived became unbearable. To remain passive and silent in the face of what was being played out before me was to subscribe.

I burst out, 'Do you think I'm gay?' Not an ideal thing to do, to a room full of blokey straight men. The world seemed to stop. 'What!?' Moo responded with sincere surprise. Looks were exchanged. Well, did I cop it from then on – if I hadn't been on the outer before, I definitely was after that. In defining me that way, the guys took the pressure off themselves. I took their taunts fatalistically. Some were more accepting than others. I was aware it wasn't an approved thing by some guys in the house, and I suppose I felt a bit belly-up at the time.

ON THE ROAD AGAIN

Life in the house was turbulent. Sometimes there were near-punch-ons, and although I felt safe, I knew they looked upon me as a different type of guy. I didn't know if I liked that any more. One of the guys walked into the room and said aloud yet quietly, 'Suck me off'. My response showed that I knew who this was steered at: 'Get fucked'.

I ran out of money. I decided I could not stay there any more. The guys, showing their devotion to a friend, all saw me off at the railway station. They joked, 'Hey, think someone's stolen your seat, better go check.'

'Really?' I replied, then realised it was their way of saying, 'We're going now'. It seemed the part of my mind that controlled logic went out the door. Things that were not funny I would find humorous. I found magic in the banal and couldn't keep conversations rolling along without finding something that would take me down another thought path. Everything that was said to me held a duality of meaning. The madness had already begun. I had no idea what was in store for me, and everyone around me as well.

URBANALITY

Banal items like aerosol cans and footballs have always held a fascination for me. This image focuses on such items, while also simplifying ideas and environment. At the time, my ideas were becoming more chaotic, so the drawing is an attempt to define and control.

THE MESSENGER

It was the festive season. I had been in Melbourne for a few months and I went with some friends to 'Rock Above the Falls' near Lorne, an outdoor festival with a stack of bands. There were a few closer friends and then a whole group of other people I had met on occasion – brothers, sisters, friends of friends. I smoked a few bongs and drank a heap over the weekend. One of the guys who was there was a bit paranoid, and the others confided in me that they thought he was losing the plot. The way they spoke of him was not overly flattering.

The friends in this group hadn't seen the suspicious and unforgiving side of me, a product of my paranoia and developing delusions. I could relate to the other poor bloke, who was more delusional than I had ever been at this stage.

I kept to myself the whole weekend, and wandered down to watch bands and add together snippets of conversation that I heard when I walked around. The environment was alive and vibrant, full of youth and energy, surely a place where one would want to be at nineteen.

Midnight came around, and the Hoodoo Gurus were playing. I had all their albums, yet the homoerotic content of some of the songs eluded me at this stage. I was sitting at the back of the crowd when a girl came and sat next to me. She was talking about Sydney and New South Wales, and I decided that she was some sort of messenger, and that I needed to follow her instructions. She seemed to know me intimately, and

A CITY
Here is visual and thematic discordance, an abundance
of symbols, and a chaotic sense of time and space
(common in people with schizophrenia).

I listened to her for a while before saying, 'I'm going to New South Wales – enjoy your night, all the best'. I had it in the back of my mind that she might report to some sort of authority figure that her mission had been successful.

ESCAPE

I snuck back into the tent and packed up my sleeping bag. I needed adventure, and I thought, 'There's no time like the present'. I was doing what a lot of schizophrenic people will do, trying to escape my chaotic mind by changing my physical environment.

I left a note for the others to find, and also mentioned that I had lost one of my rings in the tent somewhere. My friend Ang later confided in me that she thought I was giving away my possessions and might be suicidal. I was shocked to hear this. Perhaps people did sense I was discordant at that point.

Walking out of the festival with my backpack I had no idea where I was going, but I felt alive. Unpredictable things gave me a jolt of excitement, something that had been lacking in my mind and feelings for ages.

I hitchhiked to Torquay and spent a day wandering around. Everywhere I went, people's conversations were resonating with my mind, it was as if I had been touched by some magical hand. I walked through crowds of people and heard voices saying, 'Where do you think you're going now?' and 'We know where you are'. I felt uncomfortable; it seemed other people knew what I was up to, as if my adventure was predestined or predicted.

My delusions were amplified by the fact that I was by myself, and had no support to 'reality-check' with. I had no real anchor to actuality.

A RIDICULOUS PLAN

My big plan was to go fruit-picking in New South Wales. Getting a lift back to Melbourne wasn't too hard, but when I got out at Spencer Street Station I realised I had no way of getting to New South Wales. In this way, the message the girl had given me was overtaken by other more lucid thoughts.

I jumped the turnstile to catch a train back to Noble Park, as I had no money. I rang Dad and asked him to pick me up and he was surprised, as he was expecting me to be with friends at Lorne. When he asked me why I was back so early, I told him my plans. Fruit-picking in New South Wales? As soon as I said it aloud, the ridiculousness of it became clear to me. It didn't take much persuasion from Dad for me to drop the idea.

Now, years later, I will always do what I refer to as 'reality checks' with people when I feel my ideas are getting very loose. It is hard to be objective about your own mind when it is your mind being affected by illness. It's a catch-22 of mammoth proportions.

EVERYONE'S GOTTA DO IT

Back in Melbourne, I was looking for work, but not trying very hard. My degree, a Bachelor of Fine Art (BFA), we jokingly referred to as a licence to draw, or Bachelor of Fuck All. Of course there are no jobs advertised for artists. Through friends of my parents I landed a job as a storeman at the RACV branch a few kilometres from home.

Bruce, an older guy in his fifties, introduced me to the job. He had silvery-grey hair and was always immaculately presented. I liked him for his larrikin manner – he was always joking and light-hearted. I had a suspicion that he had been warned of my mental state, as I knew friends had talked about it among themselves, yet didn't ever confront me. I wondered what he knew about me.

'This is the arse-end of the place, where you will be working,' he said as we walked into the warehouse. It was my job to file insurance claims. I also had the job of hammering down staples in the corner of the paper so we could fit more files into the shelving. It was monotonous work. I was eager to please, though, and as the first few weeks went past, Bruce did less of the work and I did more. Paradoxically, I always seemed to want to please anyone in a position of authority. It's a strength and a failing; it was certainly a good way of getting high marks at school and university.

I smoked rollies incessantly, a habit I had picked up at uni, and soon formed piles of roachies where I had my breaks, just outside a roller door in an alleyway. That alleyway was to become a stage on which I communicated with conspirers that included ASIO, the police, overseas intelligence, imaginary entities and even family and friends.

> I might be ill again. I have been taking my Risperidal and Zoloft regularly. However, I am hearing voices again and I am becoming a little paranoid. Can you accept that someone could be subjected to name-calling from strangers and peers in moving cars? They have been calling me names like 'weirdo', 'weeno' and 'fag' from their cars as they pass through Burger King or as I walk along busy streets on my way to and from work or to get groceries. Can this possibly be real?
> I think the reason they are calling me weeno and fag is because they have seen me bending over looking carefully at the rocks. I am not bending over at them, I am bending over to try and find cigarette butts and

things in the rocks at Burger King. That's part of the job.
I don't want to go to the hospital again.

By the way, academically, my semester went superbly.
I earned three A's in my three classes. So I am definitely
not retarded. I am not a homosexual either. I have
200 mb of adult gifs, although I haven't looked at them
in over four years.

I am paranoid about posting this. I am writing under a
pseudonym though.

two
Disintegration

THREE PEOPLE

This image operates on several levels. It refers to close
personal relationships among multitudes of other people.
It also anticipates a ménage à trois I was involved in,
its banality, chaos and beauty.

'WE ARE FOLLOWING YOUR EVERY MOVE'

After a time I began to hate work, and Bruce sometimes got on my nerves. I got depressed and crashed out of an evening, staying up all night listening to Pink Floyd's 'The Wall'. One day I was at work, Bruce was out and the phone rang. I picked it up. 'We are following your every move,' said a voice; then nothing. Instantly the PA system from the next factory, which was quite loud, said, 'Telephone for did-you-get-that? Telephone call for we-know-you're-listening'.

I swung around and looked through the roller door. It was getting warmer and the sky was blue. I looked at the fence that separates the RACV from the factory. Was this some sort of game? I walked outside. A leaf blowing past the corner of my eye took on the appearance of a huge spider. This must be what an acid flashback is like. I motioned to the factory next door, pointing at my ear; 'Turn it up!' I yelled across the fence. Of course, no one was there. I was excited about this game, and curious about its mandates.

As the weeks passed, I got more cryptic messages. I knew that these messages were meant for me and that I had to crack some type of code to decipher their meaning.

ANOTHER CATCH-22

I had been reading a book called *Tell Me I'm Here* by Anne Deveson, about her schizophrenic son. It was on my brother's bookshelf, as he had to read it for school. I found it fascinating, and began to read over the point where someone exclaims, 'I think he's sick.'

A guy walked in to deliver some things to Bruce. He was long and lanky and seemed to me challenged in a way. I was glad he had a job – good of the RACV to employ him. He began talking to Bruce. I was quiet, looking the other way and doing my work, yet concentrating on the conversation. Bruce went out to talk to a courier. Lanky Boy walked over and said in a friendly tone, 'Whatcha reading?'

'A book on schizophrenia.'

'Is that like you?'

I hesitated. I thought about what I had been experiencing, and reflected on a recent conviction that people were *trying* to make me think I was schizophrenic. 'Sometimes,' I limply replied. He smiled and walked out. I was uncomfortable that in our exchange I was the challenged one. Deep down I knew something was not sitting right, yet it seemed ridiculous that I should get an illness I was reading about at the time. I pushed the idea to the back of my mind, yet digested the book with vigour.

At about this time I was home at Mum and Dad's. I decided to go to bed early, exhausted from what I perceived as mind games being played out by people. I was awake in the wee hours and I heard angry voices screaming abuse outside my window, hinting at things that were going on at work and among my friends. I tried to disregard it, yet I was convinced there was something ominous going on. I imagined the people out there, a few fences away so I could not track

GOLDEN MEAN

The Golden Mean of classical art and architecture gave a method of dividing up a picture plane so that the image would resolve visually. Here is a digital image of a face superimposed on a sketch of the Golden Mean; contemporary and traditional together portray angst and discomfort. The colours contrast hot and cold hues, reflecting the spectrum of possible human emotions.

them down, groups of them with megaphones, following someone's evil mandate. I prayed for a Stop button.

✉! Among other symptoms such as everything feeling unreal, inability to think straight at times, insomnia, feeling different to others, hypochondria (thinking I'm ill all the time) and irritability, I get these things where sometimes when I am a bit anxious and I'm trying to get to sleep just as I drift off to sleep I get a feeling like an electric shock and wake up with a start and my heart races and I start breathing like mad. Just the other night I was trying to get to sleep and just as I drifted off I imagined what looked like a wasp with silver wings sitting on a log. I looked at it and in a second it shot towards me and stung me, this caused me to wake up and get into a panic. Is this another symptom or is it just because I was slightly anxious and wanting to get to sleep that it happened? Why can't I be like every other kid at school? Why did I have to turn out like this? I smoked pot and so did my friends but they're fine and it's my head that's messed up. They have such hassle-free lives and they feel normal! I just want to be like I was a few years ago. Life is not fair!

ART

I found it hard to get myself together for work in the mornings, especially after staying up late into the night listening to the screaming. Mum gave me a lift one morning, and when I walked into the warehouse, I saw a painting, very like a Jeffrey Smart painting that I had studied at uni. The picture was upside down and I bent over to look at it right way up. I saw a factory and a house, connected by a field.

'Do you get it?' said a voice behind me. It was a security guard I had seen occasionally. I was surprised, trying to gather the words to address him and simultaneously realising that the painting was a symbolic gesture of communication between my place of work and my home life.

'No, I don't get it.'

We engaged in smalltalk. I decided he must be a messenger. Perhaps he knew about the speakers next door projecting messages, about the people over the back fence at night. I felt a foreboding, a sensation that objects had been placed for the ultimate purpose of teaching me something. It made perfect sense if there was a conspiracy, they would communicate ideas via something I had studied, an art piece. The security guard must have liaised with the people who sent the messages across the PA system. I decided not to confront him about it.

LACK OF INSIGHT

Later that day I was on a break. I smoked three ciggies during the ten minutes.

'Telephone call for you're-an-artist,' blared across the loudspeaker. The next line morphed into something I could not understand – 'Leva-done core uric fastness' or a word salad or rhyme similar. I was sure the first was the message, the second was to disguise the fact that a message had been sent to me. They were referring to the painting. 'Come on, you're a smart cookie,' I thought to myself. 'What are they trying to say?' Factory, work, home, look for signs at home, the answer must be there.

These kinds of wayward connections are a classic symptom of schizophrenia. They make it hard for someone who is psychotic to engage in things that might be commonplace for others. For example, I found it uncomfortable at this stage to

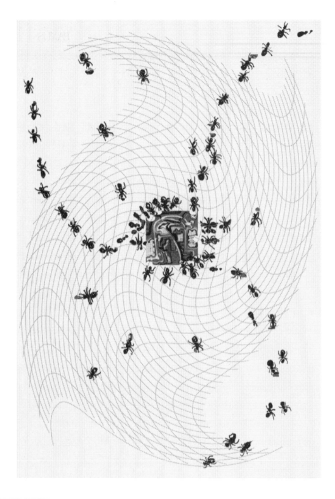

DISINTEGRATION

I think there are ways to make art out of murder, and that beauty exists in the natural cycles and disintegration of things. If you have watched a line of ants, you will know what I mean. I found I could perceive beauty in unusual things while I was psychotic. Homeostasis, or belief in opposites ('The conspirators are trying to kill me but I love them'), can be a feature of psychosis. I believe in alchemy, and in images like this I am stopping to examine and define something but also to retell it in a different way.

ILLUSIONS
Paradoxically, the product of this ugly industrial landscape, the Coke, can harbour something fertile – hence the grass growing from the can leaking 'pollution'. You can still benefit from the artificiality of delusions, even though they are not based in reality.

listen to the radio or watch television. After a spell of radio or TV I would sometimes go and lie down, out of mental exhaustion and anguish. Only then would I resolve to play music, sometimes deafeningly loud in headphones, to drown out the auditory hallucinations and escape the chaos I was experiencing. Masochistically, I often chose music that suited my frame of mind, the persecutionary homo-erotic tendencies of Pink Floyd, the channelled sexual energy of Hendrix, and the helplessness and anger of Alice In Chains. It became a case of vicariously living these emotions, as it seemed I had no capacity for expressing them myself.

Likewise, social situations were almost impossible to manage. I always came across as aloof, anxious, nervous, or just plain weird, picking up on inane snippets of conversation and asking people to repeat themselves and tell me what they were referring to.

A LEAF AND A MESSAGE

One Saturday, Dad asked me to mow the lawn, and as I was mowing the front, I picked up a frond from a pine tree. There were no pine trees around the area. There was one, however, back in Queensland where the guys were. I touched the woody foliage. Work, Queensland, home, everything was explicitly linked. I was angry that people had been gossiping to my family from Queensland. 'He's weird, a freak, he's losing the plot. He takes it up the arse, be wary of that one.'

I find it amazing now that such a bland incident could blow up in my mind to such a degree. This is a common feature of schizophrenia in that a simple stimulus like a leaf or a tennis ball can take on all sorts of implications. To others it seems as though you have totally lost it, yet I have found throughout my illness that there is a rhyme and reason to madness that people around the affected person usually will not understand.

NUMBERPLATE MESSAGES

I finished the lawn. I was going inside when a personalised numberplate on a car going past caught my eye: 'MADONE'. Thoughts ranged cryptically from the obvious 'mad one' to Ken's mother. There was a Garfield teddy at the window. I had one in my room hanging from a noose; I found it amusing. I was certain that this car had been sent to drive past so I could see the numberplate. 'I am not mad,' I thought to myself. 'They are trying to make me think I am mad. I will play their game, and I will goddamn win,' I fumed.

Already manifest in my mind was the idea that there was a whole organisation that was, for some reason, trying to bring me down. The weeks passed and I experienced similar occurrences almost daily. I began to accumulate piles of paper,

anthropomorphic

ANTHROPOMORPHIC
Schizophrenics often express themselves in symbolic terms, perhaps as a channelling of energy banked up as a result of thoughts unexpressed. This can take the shape of anthropomorphism, as in this landscape. I can remember seeing a dozen or so trolleys in a supermarket carpark surrounding another trolley, and finding in it the suggestion that I was at the centre of some clandestine activity.

recording numberplates and random 'messages' I saw or heard in the course of everyday life. My room was littered with these scraps, and sometimes I would find one that reminded me of past incidents. They all seemed to fit a master plan.

MUSIC TO MANIFEST
I listened to 'Dark Side of the Moon' by Pink Floyd over and over again. I knew it backwards, I would come home from work and it would be like a drug.

Run, rabbit run, dig that hole, forget the sun, and when at last the work is done, don't sit down it's time to dig another one.

At work I started to register that people were making comments about me as I walked past. 'Have you got it yet?' 'Shh, here he comes.'

As coincidence would have it, I found out that the guitarist from my first band worked in the big glass RACV building opposite the warehouse where I toiled. I called him, and we agreed to have lunch and catch up.

'Telephone for cross-the-road,' rang in my ears as I grabbed my brown-paper lunchbag and crossed the road to have lunch with Skeg. 'I am being tracked, someone is expecting me,' I thought. I didn't want to go over there, yet I felt I had no choice. The messages were of utmost importance, and I had to look for the next clue.

I sat down with Skeg and a few of the other workers, one of whom I recognised as an old acquaintance of my sister's. It was a frustrating conversation; every time I wanted to contribute to something I would miss my chance. I had a foreboding that this was going to be some type of social test.

Nothing I wanted to say would come out right. When finally I said, 'Hey, you know my sister,' my voice seemed extraordinarily loud, breaking the silence. Everyone at the table stopped talking as if to see what the reaction would be to my feeble comment. The girl's snarled reply was crushing: 'I wondered how long it would take before you said something'. It was obvious to me then that the conspiracy had gone further than I expected. I caught Skeg's eye. I felt he dismissed me.

At this point in my life, I felt as if I could not concentrate. I was sensitive to every nuance of social hierarchy, and talking to people was hard work. My thirst for social contact had been extinguished. My pleasure and enjoyment was always tainted by a suspicion of ulterior motives. Schizophrenic people tend not to be able to experience pleasure or joy. Even now, I could do with a few more laughs in my life. At this stage, a sliver of joy or a hearty laugh was indeed a rare thing.

WEIRDNESS ON WEIRDNESS

Looking back, I can see that my paranoia was self-fulfilling. People were hesitant about talking to me because I really was acting strangely, and their attitude to 'the weird guy that works in the warehouse' was fuel for my delusions. A few people were more accepting, yet even they seemed patronising to me. Every negative nuance in conversation hit me in powerful

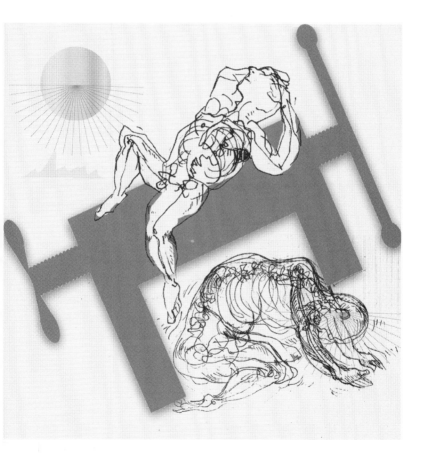

waves; and I always read multi-dimensional significances into conversation. Answering 'How do you have your coffee?' suddenly seemed a great mountain to overcome. Conversations were hard work, so I began to avoid people. I became isolated. I retreated to Pink Floyd, and heard the strangest animal sounds and screams as I lay in bed at night.

I've been in a mind room. I'd split into two persons and just one of me would go in and hang out, sit in a chair, look out the window at the ocean like a blind thing. Sometimes I'd ask a third to keep an eye on the second me I left behind, but that was probably just a stupid worry. This is true. I think what really happens is a bit of drama in the collective unconscious. I do occasionally get directly addressed by other people specifically about what I'd assumed was my private mind-space doodle. I sometimes feel like an eternal space radio, and yes, this is a serious broadcast while some other shows are absolute personal nonsense, and some people don't seem to understand the difference. Maybe they've been educated by propagandist media and they're smoking too much ganja. Anyway, all this is kinda harmless in my life. Can I go anywhere or do anything in mind-space? No. I am very careful. Do I ever need a personal guide? No. I have lots of time and nowhere particular to go because halleluya I is a bum . . . aaaaaaa a space hobo

MORE OF THE SAME

The weeks passed and I worked solidly, not really going out at all during the evenings. Bruce accepted my eccentricities, and was friendly and chirpy as always, but I felt he didn't hesitate to make the odd payout when one of his mates entered the office. Even larrikin jokes I took extremely seriously, I seemed to be way too sensitive.

I got many messages from the PA loudspeaker system and so that no one would know I was receiving the messages, I wrote them in a code that I had made up. If the conspiracy knew I could understand the messages, then they would make them more cryptic, and I was finding it hard enough to uncover the meaning as it was.

FUMBLING

A friend of mine, Rossco, was a volunteer firefighter. At a joint police/fire brigade yearly break-up that he invited me to, I had sex on an oval with a girl I knew. Originally I went for the free grog; however, when I was propositioned by this girl,

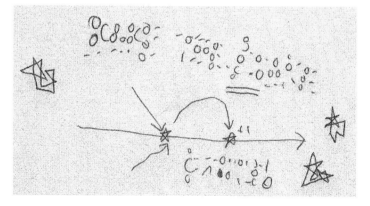

CODE

This is one of many secret 'coded' representations I drew when I first became ill. I used them to keep track of how the conspiracy was going. They were mostly 'messages' from auditory hallucinations, and I put them down in diagrams to help make sense of my distorted perceptions.

I thought 'Why the hell not?' I was not very experienced sexually. I, and I'm sure she, did not rate the experience highly. While we were buck naked next to a pavilion, and in the home stretch, our clothes laid out on the grass, I suddenly heard Rossco's voice from behind the corner: 'Rich, if you can hear me, we're hitting the road!' The voice was a real one. Timing, Rossco.

To my dishonour, I did not give the girl a follow-up phone call in the ensuing days. I was not avoiding her in particular; I was avoiding everybody at that stage.

Somehow I gathered Bruce from work had found out about it, and he slipped it into a conversation: 'A phone call saves a multitude of sins,' he said. Sex was a big issue with me at this point. It began to manifest in the messages I was receiving. I went to sleep at night with multitudes of screaming voices outside my window. One night, a voice directly outside my window bade me 'Watch your step, faggot, or we will arrest you for sex crimes'. Was it the police persecuting me?, I wondered.

The voices on the PA system started calling me a rapist. As I arrived at work, the PA system would announce, 'The snake's arrived', and 'Telephone for rape-the-snake'. I was extremely hurt and angry at this accusation, and began devising plots to curb the conspiracy.

In hindsight, of course, I can see it was a delusion blown way out of proportion. Thinking you are guilty of some hideous crime is a common symptom of schizophrenia. In reality the 'rape' was a consensual drunken adolescent roll in the hay. However, even a delusion can teach you a lot.

A few weeks later I met up with the girl again and we went to a Hoodoo Gurus concert together. Despite my making bizarre interpretations of conversations all around us, we enjoyed one another's company.

GLASS IS A LIQUID

I went with Rossco and a few friends to a quiz night that the local fire brigade/police had organised. I hadn't been out for ages. Usually I stayed shut in my room listening to CDs. The busyness of the shed astounded me.

One of the questions was 'Is glass a solid or a liquid?' 'What a ridiculous question,' I thought. The answer they gave was that it was a liquid. I thought it was a ploy for me to challenge the answer in front of everyone. As soon as I thought this, I heard such things as 'Contend it' and 'How stupid are you???' in the babble of talking people. I sank back into myself. 'It's a solid, what are they thinking?' I whispered to a friend next to me. It was the end of the night and I felt I should have stood up and queried it. The question repeated itself in my mind over and over again. The issue seemed to be of the utmost importance. Once I got an idea in my mind, it was like concrete; trying to convince me otherwise was like saying to someone, 'That chair next to you is not actually there'.

Things got rough for me in the last two years of high school. I began to get depressed and use a lot of pot to make myself feel better. I was under the illusion that pot helped me concentrate on school work, deal with people, have a good time, and to be cool. Overall I think it triggered psychosis and prevented me from keeping a job, and made me paranoid and socially inept. In high school I had quite a few friends, but I scared them off with my bizarre behaviour. I remember I was at a party after graduation. This guy was standing there and I just started staring at him. I thought he was trying to send me hateful messages and at the time he thought I wanted to fight. Luckily a friend called him off but

after that I stopped getting invited to the parties.
I began to isolate myself and think the TV was trying
to send me subliminal messages. I was paranoid and
thought the whole world was trying to make fun of
me and broadcasting information about me on the
TV and radio.

METHOD TO MADNESS, YET A BREAK FROM REALITY

Next day I was on work break, chaining rollies. I had been on
a 'G'day, nice day' basis with a few of the workers that had ciggies sometimes when I sat down outside the warehouse.

I noticed that one of the guys was reading a book on glass-
making. Last night's question was still in my mind, and it was
obvious the organisers of the quiz night had conveyed the news
that I didn't contend the answer. I took this as a message and
decided to be bold. I had had enough of voices and scamming.

'Glass is a liquid, eh?' I interrupted his reading.

'Huh?' he replied, in the tone of 'Did you say something?'
and 'What the hell are you talking about?' simultaneously.

I told him that glass is a solid and I knew everyone at the
quiz night was in on the conspiracy. He looked confused and
I sensed that I was being irrational; however, I was certain this
was a chance to get to the bottom of things. He answered,
'Right . . .' and went back to reading his book. I sensed I had
opened a can of worms and was disappointed with myself for
not having the courage to play along with the game. Now the
people organising these incidents would know I was following the clues. I walked back to work, looking over my shoulder
at the guy. He didn't look up. Then I realised the whole of the
RACV front building was mirrored glass. It all seemed to fall
into place.

TV

I have always been very critical of the media's propensity to play on people's weaknesses. Hence I rarely watch television. Yet it recurs in my work as part of my preoccupation with facades. It can also be seen as a reference to delusion. It takes a lot of work and good medication to dissolve things that seem real, yet are false.

DISMANTLING

I wondered if I would ever get to see inside the mirrored building. I decided I would have to be stronger to beat this organised persecution. I reflected that you could see into the building at night when the lights were on, and I tried desperately to think of a way that I could break the code to see in: 'C'mon, I am smart, I can do this,' said the everlasting running commentary in my mind.

At night, I played endless music, and the voices continued. I got lots of messages from the loudspeakers in the next factory in the daytime. I pretended not to notice them, while at the same time trying to crack what I thought was something cryptic, and of the utmost importance.

DID YOU HEAR THAT?

I begin to think of ways glass could be considered a liquid, and recalled that the glass in old cathedrals over the centuries slowly became thicker at the bottom and thinner at the top. I was not convinced, and went to sleep that night with voices outside my window screaming 'Glass is a liquid, glass is a liquid,' but it sounded as if they were being murdered rather than stating a 'fact'. I listened for a while, then turned up Pink Floyd's 'A Momentary Lapse of Reason'. I laughed to myself, thinking how ridiculous this had become, and reflecting that it might be some sort of human initiation. The whole world could have been prepared for my existence. This could just be my larval stage as a human.

I entertained these kinds of ideas frequently. I had a core belief in God, yet it seemed I was in purgatory. I forgave my supreme being for this, thinking that it must all be for a reason, and that everything would work out.

Sometimes psychotic people will have what is called religiosity complexes, a fascination with religion or spiritual figure. Sometimes it manifests as a good-vs-evil battle. Some think they are Jesus Christ or another such figure. I can fully understand how someone could be deluded into thinking this with the symptoms that have been described.

Many nights were dominated by the voices in my head. Most were aggressive and hateful. A few were nice or just cryptic. 'It's a clue,' an old, masculine voice screams out. I am tired, but I am awake. The voices go on for a few hours, I drift off to sleep.

Once I had been asleep, it was hard to get out of bed. I often woke and became foetal. I needed to be motionless, I needed to be more insignificant, I wanted to escape the ensuing day. I had lost my passion for waking reality. Sleeping was an attractive alternative. Simply emerging from bed was like ascending the gallows.

THE RADIO CAN HEAR YOU THINK

I was with a couple of friends, and we had gone for a drive to the beach to get stoned. I treated them as if they were friends, yet they had given me ample evidence that they were in on the conspiracy. They had been mentioning cryptic clues that related to my work, as had the radio. The PA system at work had been giving me messages that hinted at ending my life, and this resonated in their conversations.

I felt foetal. I often felt foetal. I was just going along for the ride. I had the feeling my body was just a mechanism to transport my mind to new and more devastating situations of torture. My life had lost its passion. There were things to do, people to see, yet as time went on these seemed more of a chore than anything.

Waiting outside a Seven Eleven for one of my friends, I flicked through the radio channels. I came to a station where a man was being interviewed. He was being persecuted. It was a comedy skit, but I felt the humour was cruel. Even nowadays I avoid commercial television and especially radio ads and drive-time comedy, it just seems too abrasive. 'They know I am listening to the station, know they are setting me up to persecute me,' I thought, just like this person. Something was said about a light pole, and immediately the light that the car was parked under went out. They sure were going to a lot of effort to give me messages. Transmitters, friends turning against me, family against me, remote-controlled streetlights, more messages from the radio. Every stimulus harboured a message. Helicopters overhead filled me with paranoia.

Another night I went to a friend's twenty-first at a pub. I ended up in the car with the radio on auto-search, listening to each station for half a second before it auto-searched to the next. I could even follow the songs on some stations. I had it on loud, and closed my eyes. I could make paragraphs and situations, Cyndi Lauper next to Nico, male, female, ads, news. I seemed to be creating a cross-section of contemporary culture, a rendering of my mind-set, while the party went on inside. It was cold, yet I had no intention of going back inside.

I often pulled those escape acts. Was I mad? Or was it a sane reaction to an insane world?

LONER

Instead of spending time with friends, who I felt were involved in something archaic and evil, I began to take drives down to the beach late into the night, and listen to the radio for clues. When I heard one, I gave 'thumbs up' to indicate that I had received the message, and it was OK to elaborate or move onto the next one. I wondered how they knew which radio station I was listening to. They responded to my command, and gave cryptic upon cryptic message for me to digest. I thought I could even control what they said if I concentrated hard enough.

 I'm not sure how long these should go so I will try to be concise and yet reveal as much info as possible. My wife and I have been married for almost 14 years now and she has been diagnosed with MS since 1992. Just lately she has begun hearing voices in our attic that speak to her and tell her about things that are happening that are not really happening; i.e., our 22-year-old son is dead, arrested, or in the next room (when he lives in another city). These voices and sometimes movie-like scenes are absolutely real to her and even when I disprove one of the 'statements' made by one of the voices it doesn't seem to faze her in the least.
Is a psychiatrist the only solution?

My adopted mother was severely afflicted with paranoid schizophrenia back in the 1960's and my dad divorced her and my sister and I were sent to live with her. She was very unstable, to say the least, as medication was inconsistent at best and understanding was minimal. She eventually died alone in a small apartment in ND. I love my wife unconditionally and am willing to do whatever is called for in order for her to have as normal a life as possible, but I am unsure what to do next.

FAULT

When I made this image I wanted to relate geological fault lines to a plane flying overhead – a fairly odd juxtaposition. I placed lights on top as if it were a billboard, perhaps realising that such ideas were fleeting and illogical.

CATHARSIS

I wrote a cathartic song for my first band:

Listen, listen pay attention,
to intuition,
to another element of yourself.
You may never know me in total,
by the touch of my hand
Halved I appear, united stance.
Elements of myself speak back to me
through a mirror of my mind.

Music and writing were always a source of strength, a way of crystallising ideas or opening new ideas for consideration. Performing lyrics like these also purged me of difficult feelings.

Many is the time when a lyric or piece of writing has ended up manifesting in some form, and I wonder if the dimension of time is as straightforward as we experience it. Hmm, maybe that's just a nuts way of looking at things. I get sick of neutralising thoughts that might be taking me into delusion, or suppressing ideas in this way. I feel as if I am being robbed of something.

RUN RABBIT RUN

Back at the RACV, I decided I would escape the conspiracy by going overseas with a friend, Angela. The conspiracy was making me tired and depressed. The messages threatened me, threatened my family and friends, and told me odd things from 'You are orange' to 'The phone, snake'. Sometimes they seemed to be in another language, but I had the unshakable conviction that the messages were meant for me. To this day, PA systems or bike couriers' walkie-talkies increase my heartbeat.

People were starting to realise now that I was acting quite strangely at times, doing strange things. One day, for example, I arrived in the warehouse armed with easel and ink, determined under the guise of drawing to spot the cameras I thought were in the roof, plotting my moves. I don't know what I would have done if I had seen some. I was certain that I was under observation and that there were cameras placed around the workplace to keep tabs on exactly where I was. My waking experience was bordering on metaphysical, but I still assumed that there was a terrestrial source to my experiences.

By now you may think it odd that I did not know anything was wrong, yet it is hard to make judgements about your perception when it is your own mind playing up.

POETRY

Here's a piece of writing from about this time.

I can sense you do you know my name?
I feel your eyes do you feel the same?
I try to watch you through censored eyes, censored by who?
I can wait to see your face again but I long to know your name.
You hide your subliminal messages
Through my deconstructed vision
You are beyond my realms of comprehension but you find the
time to shed your light.
If life is a sea are you my Neptune?
Is love too primitive for your constructed ways?
You are my control, you are my salvation, you are my enemy,
you are my entity.
Are you mine?
Am I alone?

ARE YOU OK?

Ang confided that people had been saying I was not quite together, and asked if I was OK. She was studying psychology, and was one of the smartest and most determined cookies I knew. I told her I was fine, and thought to myself, 'I will be fine once that plane leaves the ground.' I looked forward to going overseas, leaving the madness, leaving the isolation. Yet that was months away.

WEZ WITH A 'Z'

Wez was my best mate, always a jolly fellow. In our now only occasional evening trips about the neighbourhood in my family's Volkswagen, he often used to burst into song, waving his arms as he did so. He would burst into Deborah Conway's song, 'I'll Stand by You!', gesturing with his arms, and giggling. To this day I don't know if it was said with intent. But at the time, it made me feel good. Wez had the capacity to make you feel good. A sliver of joy, that was all I ever seemed to get.

WE'RE GOING TO KILL YOU

By this stage I was convinced that my phone was bugged and that the clock radio always humming in the background described my feelings as they happened. I felt I could converse with it, and did so for hours on end, sometimes pretending to look busy if the radio promised a clue or I felt I was on the verge of discovering something important. Always so close. So close in futility.

I had a loose sort of relationship with Bruce; he tolerated my weirdness and incessant cigarette breaks to gather the messages from over the fence. I did most of the work. Whenever he left the office I turned the radio to Triple J; when he returned he would put it back onto the races, as he read the form guide. I found this unspoken battle generally humorous, although I heard the most amazing messages when the horse races were on: sometimes my life was threatened and I was in fear.

One morning, Mum dropped me off at work. I said with a snarl, 'Don't you *dare* phone work . . .' I was convinced that people had been talking about me behind my back, I was desolately alone. Looking back, I'm sure I was worrying the hell out of my parents.

✉! My wife has just recently begun hearing voices in our attic and in the last three days has had numerous discussions with many different 'people' including some detectives (one good, one bad) who have beaten and killed some family members and seem to now run her life. She will listen to them, but not to me.
I have excellent insurance but can not find a psych doc who is taking new patients. Can anyone tell me if I can afford to wait another day (it's Sunday and tomorrow is a holiday)? I do not feel like I can leave the house. She called 911 early this am to report a killing in our attic. Please help.

ALL IN THE DIAGRAM, BRUCE

'Telephone for we're-gonna-kill-the-snake, did you hear that, snake?' boomed from the PA. Its message rocked me to the very core. I wanted to be rid of this burden. I was also angry: how dare they threaten my life! I was usually calm when I listened to these people, the pure repetitiveness of the threat lessened the impact. I was calm when I thought about someone killing me. I took comfort in the fact that the conspiracy was so huge; with so many people involved, they would not be

FLASHPOINT

I began to hold rather grim notions about the media – fast, controversial, feeding people's desires. The mystery was how something so flat and one-eyed as television could manifest in such a solid way.

Here a grim face is superimposed over a sunset scanned from a travel brochure, a sarcastic reflection on what paradise is supposed to be.

able to get away with it. I would often react in different ways to these stimuli, this time I was angered, other times reflective. 'Flattened affect' is the psychiatric term for emotional responses that are not reflective of any given situation. Clearly my responses at this point in time were characteristic of this symptom.

I drew a diagram for Bruce, explaining synchronicity and telling him how objects were sometimes placed for me to find, how messages could resonate with places I have been, things I have seen, how my mind influenced reality. I told him about the death threat.

He looked quizzically at me, and with some seriousness said, 'Are you all right?'

I explained that it was the conspiracy that was not right, and that I was going to get to the bottom of it, and that heads would roll. He asked me to elaborate. I dropped my guard and told him of the PA next door and its threatening messages. I felt as if I had betrayed myself by telling him. 'You're weak, weak,' I thought to myself. 'He already knows about it, he will not 'fess up.'

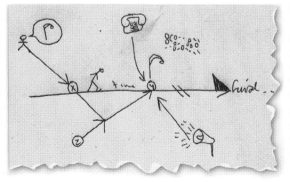

DIAGRAM

Images like this are an attempt to clear up or categorise the chaos I was experiencing. At the time, they seemed to make total sense; now, I can see that with thoughts like these I was really unable to function.

'Why do you think you are that important?' he asked.

'Don't give me this bullshit, Bruce, we all know about the conspiracy, mother-fucker'. He looked startled.

'I'm getting to the bottom of this, Bruce, straight to the source. I'm going next door to get to the fucking bottom of this right now, I'm sick to death of it,' I said quietly as I leaned over his desk. I walked out and he smiled encouragingly and said, 'Well, good luck,' trying to make light of the confusion.

I stormed out of the office and headed towards the other factory. I was deeply disappointed with myself; the conspiracy had got the better of me and I had not found a method to stop it. I was also disappointed that I had not passed the initiation. I felt sub-human. I felt I was losing a battle.

In fact, I was losing my sanity.

 I don't like what I am hearing. I sometimes think it is real, but why would someone devote so much time and energy to this? I can hear it right now. I have to go to work tomorrow. Is that funny at all?

WE BOTH KNOW WHAT I'M TALKING ABOUT

I walked through a construction site and for a moment was fascinated with the machinery and metal structures. I walked into the office of the factory next door. There was dirty carpet in there and a cheesy-looking palm tree. A woman with bleached blonde hair sat behind the desk. She was obviously chatting to a friend about her weekend. She had a rising inflection in her voice and an annoying laugh. I believed I was going to uncover something grand. I paced back and forward nervously in front of her desk. I felt excited with what I might find out.

'Hang on,' she said down the phone, then looked up: 'Can I help you?'

THE LAYERS BENEATH

This person is constructed in layers and the red line showing the guts of the matter is underneath. At the time, I was behaving in a stoic and unspontaneous manner, with my real feelings hidden – yet I felt transparent. In using black and white with strong red, I think I was trying to make sense of myself.

I said that I wanted to speak to the party responsible for the loudspeakers. She replied with another rising inflection, 'Huh?' I told her to cut the shit and that we both knew what I was talking about.

'I'm sorry?' she asked, confused. She started to look nervous. I leaned over the table and said, 'The fucking manager – *now*'.

'One moment, please,' she quickly replied. 'I'll have to call you back,' she told her friend. As she walked out the back of the office I looked at the reflection on a plastic plant, and almost forgot why I was there. I was certain the conspirators would respond to me, let me know their secrets, if I just asked them face to face.

A man in his forties appeared and said professionally, 'Hello, John Smith,' or whatever his name was. He offered me his hand, which I shook. 'I understand there might be a problem with our PA system? Can I ask where you are from, is it too loud?'

'C'mon, mate, who are you kidding, I want to get to the bottom of this,' I snapped.

'I'm sorry, I have no idea what you're talking about,' said the man, the secretary looking over his shoulder in awe.

INSIGHT

It is at moments like these that you have a flash of insight that something is definitely wrong.

I couldn't help but laugh in front of these two people, so full of confusion and discomfort. I said, 'Don't worry about it,' and turned on my heels. I cannot describe the distorted mind-set that I was in as I walked back. I felt happy that my suspicions were groundless, yet I was certain they were not telling me all I wanted to know. I was filled with so many emotions they just amalgamated into no particular one, I was monochromed.

WATERFLOW

Sexuality, barriers, invisible stimuli and influences, society, are all part of this sketch. There's a sense of entrapment in the water flow around and around. By simplifying the image, I tried to create certainty or closure around areas of concern.

IT DIDN'T WORK

I walked back to work and Bruce asked, 'How did ya go?'

'It didn't work', I replied.

'Oh well, better luck next time,' he smiled.

I sat down and another threatening message was projected from the factory next door. It filled me with dread.

I thought, 'I have just done the thing that the conspiracy wanted me to do, I showed them that I've been receiving the messages'. I felt sick with my own lack of control. I was helpless.

I looked at the clock and there were five hours to go. I felt sick with having to be there for that long. Later, Bruce told me to leave 20 minutes early, Mum picked me up and we went home. I did not relay an iota of the day's events. In the back of my mind was the belief that my parents were aware of what was going on. In any case, all I wanted was to go home and crash on my bed, and listen to Pink Floyd.

The lunatic is on the grass ... got to keep the loonies on the path.

Later that night I was having a cigarette on the back porch and I heard our neighbour say quite audibly, 'We all know about that stuff ... I've been talking to Bruce.' My whole world was tainted. I lay awake late into the night, listening to the voices.

KILL SWITCH

I cannot describe my loathing of the messages, relayed within the first five minutes of my being at work. They seemed to be in another language sometimes, and I could not decipher them, yet I had the absolute conviction that they were meant for me.

Putting away more files in the warehouse, I heard a message projected over the PA suggesting suicide. I looked down at the next file to be put away: the name on it was my surname. This seemed to carry a weight I could not bear. If I had been capable of emotion, then I would have sat down and bawled. However, my emotions over the months had been deeply buried; I was conditioned to have a poker face. I did crouch down, though, and take out my Stanley knife from my pocket. I ran the blade over my left wrist and gently broke the skin.

It was almost a relief to focus on something physical to take me away from what I had been feeling. Then I changed tack: 'Too bad if they want me to top myself – it is exactly what I am *not* going to do.'

Oh dears. I've hurt myself on purpose again. This time I grabbed a hot coal and squeezed it very hard for several minutes. Only got a 1st degree burn. Nothing serious. Only told my friend definitely not telling my parents, psychiatrist or social worker they'd be really upset or mad at me and I don't want to see that happen. Touching the fire really killed at first but then I got used to it and it wasn't so bad. Oh, gotta go now.

NO RESPITE

Back in the office, Bruce was listening to the races and looking at the form guide. I couldn't seem to block out the radio from my mind and the horse names resonated with ideas and events from the last few months. It was as if my mind was available to the broadcast. This symptom is called thought withdrawal, the feeling that ideas are inserted into your mind, or that you can be controlled by other people or entities. It is another defining symptom.

You can probably sense that at this point there is ample reason to be depressed. No wonder schizophrenia is sometimes confused with manic-depression or bi-polar disorder, and vice versa. It is often the case also, that anti-depressant medication is given in conjunction with anti-psychotics. What I needed at this stage was a monitored dose of anti-psychotics to help me regain my mind.

In my spare time I read psychology books, as if a part of me knew something was wrong. However, this self-awareness, or 'insight' in psychiatric terms, was but fleeting. When Mum said I should go to see a doctor, I just replied, 'Thanks, but no thanks, I'm fine'. It was a small indication of a great well of concern in the people around me.

I needed input to get my thoughts sorted out before dealing with the doctor. I did fax a history to the doctor with my son's permission. My son is not yet interested in his medications. He is taking them now.

Our family doctor is good and continues to make monthly appointments for my son. I am feeling low over this. My son wanted to handle the appointment on his own. Maybe I should have pushed myself in. I keep thinking that my son should deal with things on his own as much as possible.

I always find it difficult to find the balance between what I can disclose and my adult son's right to his privacy. Sometimes I find it difficult posting here. But I also need a way to maintain peace of mind and focus to get through all of this.

SUICIDAL TENDENCIES

It was at about this point that I mumbled to Mum about life not being worth living or some such comment. Mum seemed to take the comment in her stride, yet when Dad came home, he knocked on my bedroom door and said that I had upset my mother. Had they known the real chaos in my mind, they might have called for a CAT scan or something – which could have been a good thing. For anyone parallel with this state I was in, I recommend it.

Again I declined seeing a doctor in the next few weeks. Mum knew I heard voices, and treated the situation as if it

INSIDE KAREN'S BUG
Here the real is rendered with fleeting line, and delusions have the
weight of photo-realistic images. The drawing also reiterates that
there is no respite from delusion; it is with you day and night.

were completely normal. She suggested I sleep in the front
room so I could not hear them. I was grateful for her accepting attitude, but it gave me reason to believe she knew the
voices were real, so she reinforced the delusion. There is no
easy way to confront someone who is psychotic.

Unfortunately after taking 56 x 10 mg of Valium
I managed to wake this morning, what a disap-
pointment. I've really had enough of this illness and
I don't know what to try next. The last time I tried

I climbed into a tree and after placing a noose around my neck and having a last cigarette I jumped out only to find that the rope snapped, life seems so hopeless … I take my meds but it seems that after about 3–4 months I get used to them and have to try something else. This seems never-ending. I have had paranoid schizophrenia for 10 years and can't seem to see the light at the end of the tunnel, if I had enough courage I think I would just slit my throat, but I have a yellow streak running down my spine. Anyway maybe one day I will get it right. I can't talk to anyone successful because they are already dead. I've tried cutting my wrists but that was also unsuccessful. Any suggestions would be welcomed.

IT NEVER ENDS

The weeks passed, and I was quite isolated. I occasionally got out of the house to play pool with friends, but I felt I could not trust them. At home I smoked incessantly and spent a lot of time petting my dog out on the back porch and drinking coffee. Animals were a welcome relief. The voices outside my window became a nightly occurrence, and I would listen to get the next clues as to what I should do.

To an outsider, I may have come across as just shy and a bit withdrawn, and I was able to carry out my day-to-day life like anybody else. Nobody knew about the real discord in me – although incidents like the following gave people a clue.

STREETLIGHTS

I was calmly telling Shane and Wez that I could turn street-lights off and on as I passed near them. I convinced them to drive down Cheltenham Road to watch some particular lights.

Wez was stoned and exclaimed, 'I can't fucking believe it – it went off! How the fuck did you know that?' I convinced them to do another U-turn and drive-by, and it came on again as we went past. Wez thought it was hilarious. Shane jsut kept on driving. I was in unusually high spirits this day, and confided my concerns about the people who followed me about the neighbourhood and yelled abuse at me from over the back fence at my house.

When we got back to my house, I left my bedroom light off and shuffled them in. We bobbed down near the side of my bed and I said, 'Now listen'. For a moment I didn't hear any-thing, and assumed that the conspirators were being quiet because they had seen the other two enter my house. Then the silence dissipated as I started to hear the voices. Wez was stoned and crouching at my bedside. 'Hear them?' I asked. Wez, a jolly fellow, was acting as though he was on a great adventure. Then his attention lapsed and he asked, 'Can I look out?' I said, 'Don't be stupid, they will see you, it will compro-mise our position'.

I look back now and wonder how the hell I could convince them to come into my room to listen to voices, it seems so ridiculous. But there they were. Wez said, 'Well I can't hear shit.' Shane on the other hand, hushed us: 'I think I heard something'. The whole situation seems very surreal and macabrely funny to me now, and I am amazed that someone so nuts could actually convince sane people to entertain such surreal notions.

I WILL TRUST YOU IF YOU LET ME IN

I often spoke to a few select friends about 'hypothetical' situ-ations, and what they would do in them. They always reflected the situation I felt I was in, so these few people knew what I was going through. Some began to be genuinely concerned. Others were critical of my suspicious nature. By this I mean they had written me off in a way. I would often leave parties halfway through because I believed I was being singled out and persecuted. The usual pattern repeated itself: I would sit, quietly observing people chat, as if invisible. I would be utterly amazed at the parallels between their conversation and the thoughts in my own mind. It was as if my thoughts were being broadcast to them, and they were speaking in metaphor. I'd get up, walk out without so much as a 'See ya', and drive off into the night, listening still to the messages on the radio.

One night I drove madly at great speed down a dirt road, straight into a swamp at the back of Narre Warren. It was pure luck that I found a place to do a U-turn and did not get bogged. I looked around and wondered how I got there. It seemed to be symbolic of my loneliness at the time. How would I have explained to anyone that I drove a kilometre into a swamp? I thought it fortunate I didn't have to. Maybe it would have been better if I had got bogged. Dad asked the next day why there was mud all over my car, including the roof. I can't remember what I said. For my parents, clues like this started to mount up as more evidence that something was not right. I think they trod carefully.

THE STREETLIGHTS DON'T LIE

Often I would drive through suburbia and streetlights would turn off and on as I passed them. I still notice it to this day. In the past I would disregard it as a chance occurrence unless there was a simultaneous event that happened, like passing a car with a numberplate that seemed to have meaning, or a reference to me on the radio.

LIGHTPOLE

I drew this image when I was about 18, before the onset of symptoms. It amazes me that it should depict so clearly my sense of myself in years to come, and foreshadow my interest in streetlights.

One particular night I drove under about ten streetlights, and they seemed to blink off and on when I was near them. I had been watching lights for weeks as I drove around, and they seemed to get closer and closer to where I lived. I had it in my mind that the force behind this was dangerous, and I was scared of what this entity might do to me.

A painting I'd done with a streetlight in it was hung up in our hallway, and I thought that if they were manipulating things that were of interest to me, then they must have got into the house, and they could not do that unless family members let them in.

I was driving around with a friend of mine that night. I stormed home, grabbed the picture off the wall, and thrust it in Mum and Dad's faces, demanding, 'What's *this* then?' conspiratorially.

As you can probably guess, they didn't quite know what to say. They kept telling me things were just coincidental. 'You're just reading into things, it doesn't mean anything!' Mum said on numerous occasions. Of course, I didn't believe them.

OUT OF THE LOOP

Ang was one of the people who didn't know a great deal about my current mind-set. I had written off most of my other friends as enemies, but she was from a different circle of friends. I felt safe with her and was glad we were travelling together.

We would chat on the phone about places and countries we planned to visit, making bookings and saving all our bikkies. I hardly had enough for the flight overseas, but I booked it anyway. I just wanted to leave my whole life behind. Things were getting very complicated. I would often pass through the warehouse and hear someone say, 'You're dead'.

I began to ignore my perceptions and work on auto-pilot. I felt like an actor. I had to ignore my perceptions to live day-to-day. It was hard to be trusting, I trusted no one. I would find sanctuary in new people and hang out with them, as I felt they had been untouched by the conspiracy, but it was always just a matter of time before they too were one of the enemy.

WE'LL GET YOUR FAMILY

It was a Sunday, and I had agreed to mow my grandparents' lawn. I headed over in the Volkswagen, feeling OK. I was glad to see them.

After I finished mowing the lawn, Grandpa came over for a chat. He confided in me that Grandma said she heard voices from outside her window at night, and was distraught about this. Sometimes she thought he had a young lover, hiding in the cupboard. 'How dare they bring my grandmother into this?' was my immediate response.

For a second I was wracked with guilt for not being able to protect my family. I kissed them goodbye and was just driving out of the street when I saw a car numberplate that said: 'GRNMAR'. My heart skipped a beat. I drove out of their street, my mind sprinting. A car pulled out in front of me and I nearly ran into it. Its numberplate read 'CRAZY'.

I was now utterly sure that the conspiracy had gone another irreversible step. What had I done that people would want to worry my poor frail old grandmother?

I saw another numberplate saying 'DOVES' as I drove down my street. Just as I was wondering what that could possibly mean, I pulled into our driveway and saw an unusually large flock of doves on the garden path. I could just imagine people on the other side of the fence having just offloaded a box of them. Even more sinister was the idea that some synchronistic cosmic force had sent them.

I got home and told my sister of the numberplates and synchronicity and about my family being punished for my sins. She looked blankly at me. The phone rang. It was Grandma. She had forgotten to throw a tenner my way for the lawn. I said not to worry about the money and I would see her soon. 'See?' I said, hanging up. 'Synchronicity reigns supreme.' Then my sister burst into tears.

WHAT'S HAPPENING TO YOU?

I was quite shocked at my sister's reaction. She asked me to get some help, as she was very worried. I gave her a hug and said everything would be all right. It wasn't the only time that I said this to people; 'I am fine, there is nothing wrong with me' – for as far as I knew, there wasn't. At least, I didn't want to think there was.

I was convinced people were trying to make me think I was delusional. I thought I was on top of things. How different were the belief systems of my sister and I at that moment – worlds apart.

Years later I have met people who are running from treatment because their idea of being mentally ill is such a part of who they are that they don't know any alternative. It is hard to give up the idea of who you are.

 My sons are 25 and 26 and I am very apprehensive for them. 3 of my sister's 4 kids developed paranoid schizophrenia. (She and I have it as well as dad, granddad and cousins.) You're not alone.

FLINDERS STREET
If art school taught me anything, it was that people are highly individual. In this sketch of Flinders Street Station, Melbourne, each figure is connected to a clock, fitting their individual time and experience.

 I feel so much better. I stayed on the meds because I didn't want to go back to the hospital. I don't hear any voices anymore and I'm not depressed. I wish my voices were here. I miss them. Now there is just me. It's like a voice crying out in the void.

SUBVERSION HAS ALTERED

By this time, psychosis had been entrenched for so long that I'd forgotten what life was like before. I was young and vulnerable, trying to sort out sexuality, finance, employment. The knowledge that my Bachelor of Fuck All would not get me anywhere made me feel a bit useless. At this vulnerable time, I even entertained the idea that I was schizophrenic – man, would that be the easy alternative! I still thoroughly believed my delusions and incorporated them into my self-image. I was jaded and isolated.

BATTLING DELUSION WITH A PLEDGE

I felt betrayed (or at risk of betrayal) by everyone around me at this point. A bunch of us had gone out to play pool, and I invited Shane back into the house. Something he said, not available to my memory now, reinforced the suspicion that there was something clandestine going on. I immediately got a piece of paper, and wrote the following:

In regards to Rich:

There is absolutely nothing of importance or significance that I'm not letting on about and I realise friendship and honour depend on this.

Signed . . .

Then I made him read it out aloud to me. He looked quite confused by the scribbled message, and asked what it was for. 'Sign it,' I said coldly, thrusting a biro at him.

These sorts of things, I now realise, could come under the category of 'reality testing'. In making Shane sign the paper, I was struggling to strip away delusion and chaos. It didn't work. The pledge was pinned to friendship and honour, but I had no real faith that these qualities existed. He just went along with it, and my delusions remained. Looking back at my own experiences, and observing them in other people, I know that trying to convince someone their beliefs are not real is like trying to bail out the ocean with a bucket.

PRESENTATION TYPIFIES MIND-SET

At this time I had long hair, way down my back. My sister was in the bathroom doing her makeup. I saw a pair of scissors and said casually I might cut my hair. My sister didn't think I was serious, she knew I liked my hair long. On a whim, I picked up the scissors and, while she wasn't looking, grabbed my ponytail from the top and lopped it off. 'What the hell have you done?' she asked. I replied, 'Told you I'd do it.'

Well, for the next hour Mum and my sister tried to style it, but in the end we just combed it and whatever stuck through we cut off.

I think now that I was attempting to change my appearance in accordance with the changes in my persona. Since then I have read and observed that abrupt changes in clothing, shaving one's head, or uncharacteristic unkempt appearance can be an early sign of psychosis.

THE VOICES ARE THE NORM NOW

I heard voices outside my window every night now – groups of people on the other side of the fence, or maybe a few streets away so I could not track them down. They were always threatening and said the most horrible things. 'We'll kill you, mother-fucker,' 'Rot in hell,' 'We'll sort you out,' 'Had enough? – there's more,' is politely brushing the surface. One of these evenings I had had enough. I stormed into the lounge room and complained to Mum about the voices.

My parents did remarkably well in the face of such mad ideas. On the whole, though, I was not trusting enough to talk about these things with them. I suppose it was part of my general withdrawal from the people around me. I guess they had to learn acceptance, and they did it long before me.

Mum suggested again that I sleep in the front room so the voices wouldn't bother me. To me, it was as if she'd admitted she knew all about them. I assumed she thought the persecution was justified, that I did deserve such a fate, and that she had a duty as a mother to protect me. For someone who usually goes out of the way to avoid conflict, I really was in the thick of it. So many conflicting ideas.

I looked her square in the eye and said I was going to go out and find them. I did not realise at the time how pained and helpless she must have felt.

✉! I hear voices all of the time and sometimes they tell me to hurt myself. I haven't hurt myself since this time last year when I went into the hospital. I am also very paranoid. The voices tell me that someone is out to get me and they are going to shoot me in the head.
I am forty years old, and live with my mom. I cannot go outside as I am very afraid. I am divorced twice and have four grown children. They are understanding and appreciative. I have a brother who is bi-polar, so we are really there for each other.

WE'RE WORRIED ABOUT YOU

I was in my room listening yet again to Pink Floyd and trying not to hear any of the voices outside my window when Mum came in and tried to convince me to go and see a doctor. I said something along the lines of 'Nah, Mum, I'm really all right, I don't want to see a doctor'. I could always pull myself together in order to escape conflict. I didn't want to upset her, but I wanted her out of my room all the same so I could be by myself. I wanted to sort myself out, I wanted to have people around that I trusted, yet I wanted to be alone, I wanted people to drop in, I wanted to understand what was happening to me. Had I known what was going to happen, I would have taken Mum's suggestion immediately.

By this stage I was convinced that because I had read a book on schizophrenia, people were trying to make me think I had it. If I were to go and see a doctor, then it would mean the conspiracy had won. There was no way I was going to let that happen. So I was adamant that I did not need to see a doctor; indeed, I was quite abrupt with Mum. Doctors: definitely not.

BETTER GET A LAWYER, SON

As I had been in the band scene for a few years, I liked to spend time in pubs seeing Jimi Hocking, Seaweed Gorillas, and bigger bands like Midnight Oil. One night I found myself next to Tex Perkins, singer from The Cruel Sea. I did not talk to him, but soon after that I heard their new single, 'Better Get a Lawyer': another sign.

I was quite astonished that a song would be written about me, but fully believed that it was. I bought the single soon afterwards, holding it up in the air as I left the record store just so that those following me could track my progress. I wanted 'the Conspiracy' to be aware I had received the information intended for me, so that we could both establish more direct communication, and maybe resolve things.

TELEVISION SPEAKS

I began to look at the media as another channel of persecution. Why not? By now everyone I knew was involved in the conspiracy; of course they would get media people in on the act.

As I went through the lounge room, I saw Rex Hunt, fisherman extraordinaire, on the TV, saying that I had fucked everyone over and was now leaving the country. Fucking oath I was leaving the country, I said to myself – anything to rid myself of this burden that enveloped me.

I was really upset the other night because the people on the news were saying what my thoughts were. I know this is true because they sent me messages on what they were doing. I hate it when they can tell my thoughts to everyone who is watching them. I also hate it when people can hear my thoughts and know everything about me.

What did I do to deserve this? I never asked for schizophrenia. It just came without my permission. All I want is the powerful force and the voices, nothing else.

I don't want to be paranoid, depressed, full of anxiety, pain and sickness and all those other psychotic symptoms.

I'm kind of excited because I'm going to see *A Beautiful Mind* when it comes to theatres in Owen Sound and of course I have a lot of regression and bizarre behaviour and I'm still hearing those funny voices. Some are very derogatory, and others are nice.

ROMA PRESENTATIONS

I was working again, listening to the messages and avoiding conversation with Bruce. Walking through the mobile shelving, I got up to 'R' and the second I read a bit of writing on the folder, the loudspeaker across the fence confirmed there was a message in it. Then I realised it was in my father's handwriting. Why on earth would my father write 'Roma Presentations' on the folder? It must be a clue.

I went back into the office and out of the blue, Ang suddenly rang. She said that due to a booking error, we would get a 26-day tour in Europe for the price of a 20-day tour. I was happy to hear it, and asked where were the extra stops. 'Rome,' she said, rolling her 'r's as if she had just seen an appetising dessert.

So now the conspiracy was leaking into my overseas plans. I was wary of Ang now, although I truly believed that she had no part in the conspiracy yet, that it was the work of people bugging the phones and tracking my moves.

Later in Rome another coincidence would occur: I began a travelling romance with Kylie, a pretty blonde woman from Western Australia. She knew psychosis all too well: she was a psychiatric nurse.

✉! Late last August my wife had an acute episode that lasted 7 weeks where she had delusionals, hallucinations and extreme paranoia, she was scared to her very soul. She felt everyone was out to get her and kill her. She thinks 'they' got me and implanted a chip in me and now control me to work against her and to kill her. She tried burning fish incense in our house and spreading holy water from the church to cleanse us. She called the police to report all the people following and watching her.

She has refused any and all meds her doctor gave her to reduce her symptoms. She has filed for divorce because I am controlled by Satan and she cannot be married to me.

I talk to her every day and see her occasionally but always ends up that I am out to kill her and that Satan has me etc. etc. to the point where my patience wears out and I break it off just because I can't take it anymore. I don't argue with her or deny her beliefs but she just won't let them go. And the sad part for me/us is that maybe she never will. You can't disprove or argue with delusions or hallucinations.

All I can do is stand by and pick up the pieces. It's so sad to watch something beautiful go bad and not be able to do a thing about it.

A FRIEND'S VOICE

I remember one night hearing the voice of an old university friend, Amanda, saying 'Rich, your Dad's got cancer,' right outside my bedroom window. I felt somehow guilty about this. Years later, she called out of the blue. That same week we found out Dad had to have skin grafted from his neck to his nose – quite a big operation. I often wonder whether events like this have any meaning at all. It is often hard, even when you have recovered, to see falseness or delusion when you have experienced it as real.

POETRY

I was always writing snippets of prose or poetry on bits of paper. This one shows some of what I was feeling at the time.

You are part of me not because I know you,
but because you exist.

There lies potential in strata of chance and destiny,
to meet you face to face.

You can't hide the light of your soul from me
by simple physical boundaries.

We breathe the same air,
live under the same sky.

You are me, I don't want to kill you, I can learn
from you in ways you would never expect.

CATCHING MUM AND DAD

Often when I was with someone, when I turned my head I would hear their voice saying cryptic, ominous things. When asked 'What did you say?' they would invariably say 'Nothing'. I was forever trying to catch people out and never succeeding. The voices in the back yard would never materialise when I placed microphones outside my window to record them. Astonished that they would never repeat themselves with a tape rolling, I would then search my room for cameras.

Eventually my suspicions spread to Mum and Dad: the night voices began screaming that I should move out, that my parents hated me. I was crushed at the thought and forced myself to put the curses to the back of my mind when I was talking to Mum and Dad. Just as I thought what it would be like to have them yell out at me through the darkened house, they did. The only thing I could think of was to catch them in the act.

The only way to do it was to be on the other side of the door when they yelled stuff at me, then bust them. There was a problem, though: the glass doors of the family room were in full view of the 'people' on the other side of the fence, and I didn't want them to track my moves through the house.

I can relive the experience now as macabrely funny. I am under my doona, crouched down on the floor, like a turtle, and I am going to bust Mum and Dad's cover by confronting them when they yell abuse at me. Slowly I inch my way across the floor. I take a peek out the window and see our dog cowering at the door as he often did. My breath makes puffs of vapour in the cold and the moon is near full. I get across the doorway then do an army roll into the kitchen, complete with doona cover.

Then I hear Dad's distinct and clear voice: 'He's in the kitchen'. How did he know? The only possible way was via his bedside radio, which had to be connected to ASIO.

I am exhausted, I am alone, I am on the kitchen floor hugging my doona. 'Cunt,' outside voices scream, 'Kill yourself,' they scream. Aha, this is the test – they can't kill me so their plan is to make life so hard for me that I do it myself . . . I am instantly stoic: nothing will break my spirit, I am fucking going to win this test. They know I am in the kitchen now, so I just walk back to my room. I give them the bird as I walk past the glass doors. I listen to the abuse for an hour or so, then turn up the stereo so I can't hear them. I sleep exhaustedly without dreaming. When I wake up, I fantasise about being somewhere exotic and far away, where no one could know me.

YOU WANT THE CAR?

My parents' Ford was stolen, and I began to hear messages associated with it. My general feeling was that I was not passing the tests set for me, and as a consequence my parents were beginning to suffer. I even wondered if Mum and Dad had agreed to this car-stealing as a test of my loyalty to them. The

HOUSE
This image of a house and things around it suggests discordancy by virtue of the perspective changes. Yet the strength of the containing line suggests a controlling principle that might bring all these disparate things together is still available.

voices said they were going to tell me how to recover it.

As in the incident with my grandmother, I was depressed at the thought of people I loved being brought into these scenarios. I was racked with guilt, and felt I was a burden. I could trust no one.

I was driving in the Volkswagen not far from my home, and a voice said on the radio, 'Turn right for the Ford'. I was astonished at the clarity and purposefulness of the message. I decided that if I ignored the message they would have to give me a more obvious one that I would be able to record or store in some concrete way, confirming my suspicions of a grand conspiracy. I was still convinced that I could catch them out, I daydreamed that maybe I could sue them.

I decided not to follow the command, but was certain the message was accurate in telling me where the car was. I felt guilty that my parents knew nothing about the car, and that I was doing them a disservice by not responding. Then again, if Mum and Dad were in on the plan and they knew I was not letting on where the car was, all the more reason for them to join the other side. I felt trapped. In retrospect I curse my vivid imagination for dreaming up such myriad complex ways for me to be persecuted!

THE CAR IS RECOVERED BEFORE YOUR MIND
A week later the car was found behind a McDonald's store, not far from where I received the hallucination, funnily enough. The police talked to Mum and Dad and it was revealed that guns were being sold out of the boot, or that guns were somehow involved with the stealing of the car. I thought it was a hint that the conspiracy was threatening murder, with me number one on their hit list. I pushed the idea out of my mind in moments of clarity.

LOGIC OUT THE WINDOW
I reflect that when I was delusional, I felt the part of me that controlled logic just went out the window, and things that seemed ridiculous to other people or indeed myself at this present time, seemed totally real, unquestionably true.

At this point I should say that the whole time these 'events' were going on, I was still mixing quite sociably with my family and friends, and most of the time they seemed to be quite accepting, however bizarre my comments were from time to time. Once when I complained about voices outside my window to Mum, at a stage when I still trusted her, she suggested that I put my stereo further from my bed, as the electromagnetic waves might be affecting me. I dismissed the suggestion as ridiculous, having a core belief that the voices were real. It seemed I wasn't the only one looking for the reasons the way things were as they were.

I DON'T HAVE TO PUT UP WITH THIS

I was feeling very low by now, still getting a daily barrage of messages at work, and they were getting me down, lower than

Doodling on the computer on a lucid day produced this. The first pictogram defines a streetlight with a message, the second indicates the anxiety I felt when that was happening. The third shows how spoken words morphed for me into something different but phonetically similar. The numberplate on the car says 'weknowhereuare'. The picture also suggests my (fading) insight that these things were facades, shown up by the scanned sunset in the background.

I had ever felt before. However, I could still put up a mechanical facade for my daily work life: nice day, not much rain of late, farmers won't be happy . . .

One morning I walked into the RACV and opened the big roller door. It was a cold windy morning and leaves were blowing in the door. The PA system said, 'Ready for another day, cunt?' I looked around the warehouse for cameras again, looked at the speakers perched up on poles next door, wires running to somewhere important. I would have liked to drop to the floor and bawl. However, months of torture had driven my emotions literally underground beneath a stoic surface. I thought, 'I just can't take this any more; I have no one I can trust, and fuck this conspiracy, I feel as if I am in a labyrinth. I need to escape'.

Bruce was not at work yet. Hoping I wouldn't run into him on my way out, I left the RACV forever. I crossed the Princes Highway, heading home, for want of a better place to go. Two men working in a front yard caught my eye as I walked past. They were saying, loudly enough for me to hear, something like, 'We will follow you wherever you go and make life hell for you'.

EVEN GOD IS IN IT

The conversation I overheard may well have been about the footy, but I took it as more evidence of how far the conspiracy was prepared to persecute me.

I was awed by how clever it was. Ironically, this respect for the intelligence of the conspiracy allowed me to read more meaning into common conversation, or mundane events. A newspaper blew in front of me and the headline seemed inexplicably linked to my situation. I got to the point where not only people were in on the conspiracy, but I could see hints of something God-given or organised.

I am not surprised at all when I read that some schizophrenic people believe for example they are Jesus Christ, or some other spiritual figure. The world can speak to the psychotic person in many ways through analogies, metaphor or symbols. Not long ago I did an IQ test, with varied results: in maths I got 8 per cent, in analogies I got 95 per cent. It makes me wonder if there is a predisposition for a delusional personality.

I'LL HACK IT BECAUSE I NEED THE CASH

If I was going to make it overseas to escape my horrible and exhausting existence, then I needed to save as much money as I could. I had frequent conversations with Ang about how much we had saved up, and she was leagues ahead of me.

I had many jobs in this time. The most humorous to me, looking back, was delivering high-class cuisine from restaurants to houses in affluent suburbs. Dressed in a tuxedo, I would pick up flounder and lobster in our beat-up old combi van, and deliver it to mansions in Toorak and South Yarra. To confirm delivery, we had a CB radio system linked with the base in Glenhuntly. Well, you can imagine the voices and delusions that I experienced through this walky-talky gadget. And in a weird twist, I really was being tracked through the suburbs.

As I drove around, listening to messages from the CB and radio, I would invariably get lost. Looking back I'm amazed I didn't have an accident. A five- or ten-minute delivery might take me an hour. I read meaning into the names of streets I was sent to, again confirming delusions.

BON APPETIT

At one stage I had to brake suddenly, and a piece of flounder on a silver platter ended up upside down on the floor of the

Volkswagen. I tried to recover it as best I could. When I got to the house an hour later, because I had got lost, it was cold and had sand through it. The bloke inspected it at the door, realised it had been spilt and had a few stern words to say to me. As we stood on the porch, his door slammed shut in the wind; he was locked out. He was screaming and cursing, but the whole situation seemed hilarious to me, so I laughed and wished him a good night. When I got back to the base, I was fired. I didn't mind, I was using more petrol than I was earning anyway. It seemed impossible to get some cash together at this point.

CHASING PLANE FARES

I took many jobs through casual work agencies, packing, filing papers and filing metal, banging pallets together, and all the time the conspiracy followed me. At one place I thought they were trying to make me believe there were small monsters in the air-conditioning units, by rattling them from the other side of the wall. 'How stupid do you think I am,' I used to think to myself.

I was very depressed, and my communications with people often ended in a stigmatised reaction. It was only through herculean efforts that I could drag myself up into being an apparently 'normal', sociable person.

COINCIDENCES

About this time I was at the local shopping centre, thinking about going overseas. To my surprise a man walked aggressively in front of me, and put his arms out as if he were a plane and zoomed in front of me making a plane noise as he went. Was it a message telling me the conspiracy knew I was going overseas? Now I wonder if it really happened. To this day there are a lot of incidents whose reality I'm uncertain of. If those events didn't happen, what remains for me of those years of my life?

At the time, I suppose, I just learnt to live within a high level of uncertainty.

I have never figured out if what I went through was real or not. I thought I was chosen to do special things. My mission was to kill the devil and rid mankind of evil. And some of the things that were told to me to this day scare me half to death just to think about it. I mean it frightens me out of my mind what I was told what could happen if I failed. I use thought blockage and medication. Curious to know how many people still think some if not all of their hallucinations were real.

SWING
The Internet provides great resources, support and freedom for its users, as the emails in this book attest. The person on the swing here has found freedom in this electronic landscape.

three
Surreal Sojourns

The day had come for our flight overseas. Ang and I were excited, and I for one was glad to be leaving my past behind for a time, even though Mum was crying. It was a long flight and I got slightly sloshed, so much so that I had to ask a different stewardess for another suburban and Coke. We slept for a while and arrived at Athens.

We had a big trip planned, lasting three or four months. We were to see Greece (including the islands), Turkey, England, Scotland, and continental Europe. I was happy that everything was exciting and new. Little did I know that Ang had been warned by friends to be wary travelling with me, they said I had been losing the plot. Ang is warm and intelligent, and takes obstacles in her stride, but in time she too would find my illness difficult to confront every day.

One of the reasons we went to Greece was to catch up with my old university friend, Kirsten, who was working there as a nanny. By coincidence, Ang had gone to high school with her. The messages at the RACV would sometimes mention Kirsten in different contexts, and our relationship was tainted by my delusions. Now she is a soulmate; she still drives me nuts, but I love her to bits.

LONDON IS SCARY

After a week in Greece with Kirsten, Ang and I flew to London to stay with Ang's friend Sally.

All my time in London I felt I was being followed, and there were many instances where I got 'messages' from various sources, radio, TV, street press, that seemed to have intimate connections with how I was feeling and the life I had left behind. They also connected with things that would happen in day-to-day life. I was quite amazed at this and decided that I really must have been an important person to have this happen. I fluctuated between delusions of grandeur and delusions about being persecuted, and chaotic combinations of the two.

I had read a book called *Bravo 2 Zero*, by Andy McNab, about the Iraqi war. Sally had been handling faxes from the author at work, which she was excited about, as she had read it as well. Enter a new idea: the UK equivalent of ASIO had been informed of my presence in London. Suddenly the threat of being on someone's hit list became much more real.

METAPHYSICAL FODDER

Meanwhile I was meeting new people, being out and about town on the Tube, having coffee with people I met in laundromats. I was ostensibly friendly, but my paranoia was always just below the surface. I often asked people what they knew about private detectives and directed conversations towards such esoteric subjects.

VICARIOUS EMOTIONS

I was catching the Tube back from Camden Market when I began to be curious about a lady who was sitting opposite me. I noticed her initially because she kind of made a 'guffaw' noise. I looked away for a second and heard her say something along the lines of 'It's your fault.' It was then I realised she had burst into tears, and was trying to compose herself. I looked up, and it seemed she could stare straight into my core. Instantly I thought of British Intelligence hiring out actors to dock with moments of my day, picking moments when I was alone, and unable to share or reality-check the experience with anyone.

The sky was grey, and the train was quite empty apart from a couple of other people. As we rattled through the suburbs, this woman was having a profound effect on me. If I'd had the capacity to cry I would have wept with her. But for this moment all I could do was look into her eyes, realising that it

BUGS

One of my beliefs was that a race of beings had liberated the soul from three-dimensional reality and time. They were observers of space-time. Sometimes I felt I was touched by these beings, or felt their presence around me.

The containers are a childhood toy, the 'bug catcher' that I received as a present in my childhood. The advanced beings clustered around them are observing the artefacts of human technology.

Years later I realised that the sign at the bottom said (in my own secret code), 'Have you lost the plot yet? Is it time to go home?'

was my fault she was upset. She seemed symbolic of the environment of my mind, I vicariously became her. I wished I could take back my staring.

COLD WATER

It was quite chilly in London at this time of year, and as bad luck would have it, the hot-water service in Sally's place had packed up. I instantly saw this as a ploy by the conspiracy to make me have cold showers, forcing me to to wake up to myself. As I surveyed shops and sites around London, things that affected me personally like the cold showers were reflected in the messages I heard from people around me. If I thought someone was a part of the conspiracy, and could give me information, I would follow them around a store or up the street, listening for clues. Sometimes I struck up surreal conversations with people.

At such times I would have moments of insight and think how ridiculous my daily life had become. Yet the delusions had a potency that I was unable to dissolve, and I would slip back into my beliefs in a second.

A WELCOME CONFIDANTE

We spent the best part of two weeks in London, and slowly I confided in Ang my daily experiences as we went about town and chatted about the house. She was and is a good listener, and I was glad to have her with me at the time.

We became quite chatty and had a closeness that I appreciated. We talked about everything from mental illness to politics and sexual experiences and fantasies. She was warm and accepting, and sometimes she joked about me being a mad bugger, which lightened the whole issue, then we would swing to serious discussions in which she was trying to understand what was happening to me. Sally was a nice woman as well, and very accommodating, yet she knew nothing of what I was going through as far as I was aware. In the two weeks I was there I thought on many occasions that she was giving me cryptic messages.

One day the phone rang unexpectedly and it was Mum from home. I was happy to speak to her, and she asked if her letter had arrived. Two seconds later, as I looked at the front door, the postie delivered it through the mail slot, and for once I didn't feel there was a reason or planning behind it, that it was just pure coincidence. Later on I was going into town to meet some people and a car went past me with its window open. I could hear snippets of my conversation with my mother earlier that day. I reneged on my lack of suspicion.

I longed to know why these games were being played. Who was playing them? Why? I began entertaining the idea that these games were not from a terrestrial source; my paranoia hinted to me of something more metaphysical or God-driven.

A LOST DIARY ENTRY

I recently found a scrawled diary entry from that time, trying to make sense of my situation:

> *Even the two Australians seemed to know details about me and muttered smart-arse comments under their breath to me, then I would ask them to repeat it and they would say something totally different. More evidence. Even as I write this it is happening. The people next door seem to be talking about me and yelling things out. And I just read that wearing headphones can phase out or distract from voices in your head. I put them on and can still hear things. But they could have been people next door. When the song finished I could hear*

what was going on more clearly, someone said 'He's tripping out' as if they knew on cue when the song would finish. Dammit, who am I kidding? For months I couldn't wait to get out of Australia so I wouldn't be persecuted.

They were in the back yard at night, followed me to every place I worked, broke into my car and I'm pretty sure they had my phone bugged. How else would they know to follow me around and put stuff on numberplates for me to see?

Like the time Ang and I went to Frankston, and after we spoke on the phone about our French visa, the words 'LUNDI', French for Monday (which it was) was encountered in our drive there, then the numberplate 'WURDS' after it. You don't have to be too over-associative to realise they aren't normal car numberplates.

I feel like I'm at the fool end of the world and its fucking court jester. I'm not willing to go through life feeling like this.

What's more, I know I haven't been thinking right. And I also know for absolute certain that there is a scam against me. Maybe it's not as serious as I thought but its vastness is encompassing. I'm caged. Everywhere I go, people seem to interrogate and oppress me. And I see them. I see them on the streets of London with their mobile phones. And the telephone bloke coincidentally fixing some wires whenever I turn up to a new place. The sheer paradox is that his presence says, 'Yeah, we're gonna get you,' and I haven't got a leg to stand on. Brood.

I hear them in the streets too. It was in Melbourne, Dandenong, London: 'Yeah, that's him'. And persecuting me from loudspeakers as I walk past. I know for a fact they did it at work, and even when I walked down Cheltenham Road. It happened about four streets away today. And it happened in Chadstone and in Jodie's work. Specifically in Katies! The fucking nerve of them, turning my sister against me. My friends, my family. And they all act ignorant of it all.

And they have the nerve to yell stuff out at night and say cryptic phonetics to my face and still act ignorant.

Then again, how can 200 incidents a day be planned? I know some I have reality-checked and they have been false. Sometimes I can feel the ground move – like a jolt and I have to get my balance. Sometimes, like right now, spaces can move and my centre of balance can seem to pull to the left although I can still stand really easily. But that hasn't happened a whole lot lately.

It's strange, every now and again the whole thing seems so incredibly ludicrous and the only reaction I have is to laugh. And I can't help but chuckle absurdly.

SELF-MEDICATING

I had met a few people from the laundromat, including a good-looking woman with long black hair and a cute South African bloke who was staying with her. We were all to go out on the town. I think they perceived me as shy, and they promised a good night with knowing looks to each other. In the back of my mind I fantasised what a good night with these two might encompass.

We were going to a club in central London called SW1. They checked everyone's chewing-gum packets before we entered, which caught my curiosity, and it was fairly packed when we got in there. We had met up with some of their other friends and I was going to get a drink when one of them said, 'You wont be needing that'. In her hand was a pill, Ecstasy, that I had always been curious about. The thought of being on a chemical high in the face of my current mind-set was inviting. I thought of my day-to-day life, and reflected on my endless attempts to escape it. I was curious as to what its effect would be like. There was only one way to find out. I swallowed the pill.

An hour later it started to kick in, and because the music was too loud to really understand what people were saying I just danced and danced to my heart's content. People were smiling and having a great time and I felt waves of pleasure through my body. People were beautiful, I enjoyed looking at everyone dancing and for a while felt exalted. When it started to wear off, I was disappointed the effects didn't last longer. I located a dealer and bought a whole other pill for £12. I took another half.

I was OK for a while, and danced as I never had before. It was around 9 a.m. by the time we left the club and sat at Victoria Station having coffees. In this wired state, in an unfamiliar environment, and with the comfort of loud music gone, the real world suddenly presented itself to me – slick, shiny, surreal. I found it hard to carry on a conversation and was having definite audio-hallucinations. Ecstasy was surely a bad choice for me, and I advise people in the grip of psychosis, or disposed to psychosis, to tread very carefully.

It was hard to keep on track with the conversation. I retreated into aloofness, the disguise I adopted when trying to elicit secrets from people. The familiar hierarchies became apparent. I couldn't bear to be in these people's presence for much longer. I thanked them for a good night, said I had to get going, and disappeared into the bustling crowds of Victoria Station, a wired and psychotic loner.

I went past a shopping area near Camden Market, and read the most amazing secrets into the passing conversations. I remember helping someone down some stairs with boxes and luggage, until I felt my life was being threatened again, and I found myself power-walking to a park for some respite. It was about midday, and all sorts of people were sunbaking in foldout chairs in the park, which I found ridiculous as it was not that hot compared to a Melbourne summer. I wandered around for a while, finding humour in flabby white torsos.

Even in the face of the morning's delusions, I felt that I had had a good experience the night before, deciding Ecstasy was not all that bad. Those few hours of physical movement and no words left me feeling I had got rid of a lot of pent-up feelings.

The next few days, however, were a bit of a test.

PLANTS
I've always been interested in nature, and deplored the corporate obsession with palm trees. Here's a group effort (perhaps also a conspiracy?) to pull apart a facade and reveal the truth of biodiversity.

ADVERTISING SECRETS

I had picked up a street press publication, and in it was a curious advertisement for shoes in a design that somehow led me to believe they were referring to Kirsten and myself. I called the number on the ad when Sally and Ang were out and said, 'Hi – I'm the bloke that your ad is based on and if you think that I'm going to see Kirsten again you are right, I have a plane booked back to Greece in a month'. I got the response you might expect. My delusional thoughts were neutralised, immediately.

HEADING NORTH

Sally and Ang were fairly close friends, and they decided to go to Belgium for a couple of weeks. On a spur-of-the-moment decision the next day, I packed my backpack and went to Victoria Station to get a bus to Edinburgh. I had always been curious about the country, as my ancestors were Scottish. I walked the now-familiar streets through Kensal Green to the Tube, and got to Victoria Station on the cusp of a great adventure. Despite my ongoing symptoms, I felt free and confident in the face of solitude.

EDINBURGH

Walking through Edinburgh for the first time, I found that the conspiracy had followed me all the way there. Projected from high up in a building's facade came the familiar sounds of shrieked accusations, insults and unintelligible screaming.

CONVICTION

Readers may find it hard to believe that I would actually think these voices were real, but my psychosis happened so gradually, and affected my insight and logic to such a profound degree over time, that the delusions I was experiencing were unquestionably true for me.

Anyone who has known someone psychotic, or has been psychotic themselves, may identify with or confirm this unshakable belief.

THE BLUE BANANA

I spent a couple of days seeing the sights of Edinburgh, taking in galleries and the Royal Mile, and fossicking through bookshops. I bought a stack of art books at a sale which I then had to carry around with me, much to my discomfort.

HOSTEL
The hostel I was staying at was an old converted cathedral, and there was a lot of sport on the communal TV. I sat at a distance most of the time, drawing the scene and writing messages in code in my sketchbook.

At one stage a few acquaintances and I became a travelling team, and we would plan to catch the same bus to the next point on our tour, called Blue Banana tours. I got on well with these three, and to my relief, my delusions started to fade and the hallucinations slowed down.

One morning I was supposed to get up early to go rock-climbing in the Cairngorm Mountains, but I slept in. I often found it a tremendous effort to get out of bed (lethargy is one of the 'negative' symptoms of schizophrenia). That morning I missed the bus. I wandered through Avimore, drinking two Red Bulls, energy drinks saturated with caffeine, simply because I was thirsty and they were in my backpack. I ended up hiking to the top of the Cairngorms, where I met an English bloke about my age. We talked superficially, but there was a strong sexual tension between us. We were alone, horny, and both willing. As I came on the top of those mountains, three gunshots went off in the valley below as if synchronised with the event. I felt instantly as if I was being watched, and that my whole life was being recorded, which nowadays I believe is true, metaphysically.

I often think that my bisexuality played a big part in causing stress at this stage in my life, and that it contributed to my psychotic episodes. I think sexuality is a big issue for many young people, and have heard it still plays a role in the very high Australian youth suicide rate. It doesn't surprise me. Sexual references, stemming from underlying guilt and unresolution, would often manifest in my delusions.

PROMISE ME

Back in Edinburgh after a sojourn for two weeks in Inverness, my other friends departed and I was again on my own for a week. I was aware that I should have taken advantage of my

OBAN
A straightforward, meditative sketch,
one of many I did on my trip.

time in such a place, yet more often than not I would sleep until early afternoon. I think it was a combination of being thoroughly exhausted from all the stimuli I was exposed to every day, and the fact that I would stay up late at night all the time, hanging about in pubs and nightclubs, drawing and/or scribbling secret messages in my code.

I still had half a pill of Ecstasy in my pocket, and as I was out one night talking to a few people around a table, I decided on the spur of the moment to pop it. One girl was from the same hostel I was staying at, and we ended up hanging out and I walked back to the hostel with her. On the way back I revealed some of my thoughts, she asked 'Man, are you on drugs?' I said yes – and then, throwing caution to the winds, confided in her my suspicion that people had followed me from Australia, and that Scottish Intelligence knew where I was staying, I asserted that the universe has an order, encouraging synchronicity to reveal secrets. After a while, she realised that I was actually serious, and that my belief in these things was unquenchable.

By this stage we were back at the hostel playing pool, and there were people up watching music videos. We played and chatted for a while, with me 'shushing' her at various points so people who might want to infiltrate the conversation could not hear us. Even in that state, I was worried about what other people might think, probably a subconscious awareness that my ideas were way off target. She was leaving the next day. She made me promise that when I got back to Australia I would go and talk to a professional to sort out my ideas. It was a promise broken.

A WALK, AUGUST 1994

That night I went for a walk, and ended up running from imagined hit-men, crouching in an alley, listening to the voices from my mad mind. In retrospect I see it as a defining point: I really was psychotic with absolutely no insight into my own mind. I would not wish such an experience upon a worst enemy.

I KNOW YOU ARE FROM ASIO

I slept till about two in the afternoon one day. When I finally woke, as good fortune would have it, the Edinburgh Festival was on and there were plenty of things to see and do. I remember at one point climbing up a tower in a park, via narrow

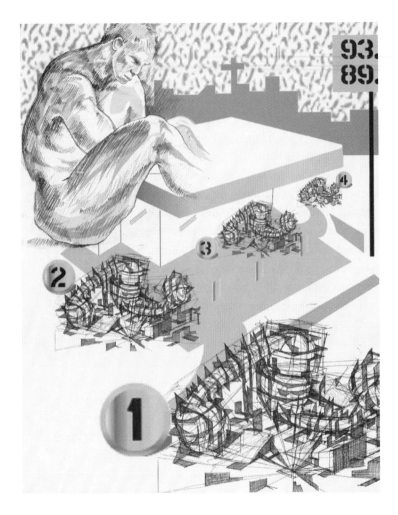

PETROL STATION

Years ago I did a drawing of two telephone receivers linked
together. In retrospect I see the homoerotic element in this,
but it didn't strike me at the time. The mechanical nature of
many casual sexual encounters is also part of it. Like a car
getting petrol, there's a beginning, an end, and the job is done.

spiral stairs, and looking out very small windows into the surrounding landscape. Near to the top, the stairway got even narrower, and people would have to give way to let each other up and down. I got caught up the top with a surge of people entering below and I wanted to scream. When I got out I walked into the park swinging my arms around. I fought the urge to run aimlessly.

I had learnt that if I had my headphones on really loud I could block out the voices. I put on Soundgarden's 'Superunknown' album, and I dossed down in the park at the base of the Royal Mile.

When the tape finished, there was silence, and I heard someone behind me say something about keeping tabs on me. I was startled by its clarity and listened closer for any clues. I must have stayed there for half an hour, occasionally glancing at a couple behind me. The trouble was, every time I turned around, they would just sit there, not saying anything. Every time I turned away, I would hear them hurl threats and insults.

I had had enough of this constant jabber. I decided to confront them about it.

It was a warm day, there was a Ferris wheel nearby with kids playing and tourists from all over the world enjoying the sights. Above was Edinburgh Castle on top of its volcanic structure, archaic and old. I took a deep breath.

The woman was lying down resting her forehead in her hands, sunbaking. I wandered over slowly and sat down, right next to them on their small picnic blanket. They looked alarmed as their space was invaded.

'Hi,' I said.

The man looked a bit perturbed, the woman looked up, and it was then I started the small talk, nice day, where are you from – to see if they would give away any clues. Once that proved futile and they were getting uncomfortable, I felt confident I had caught them out. The conspiracy would never, judging from past experience, expect me to track down persecutors and drill them. As I was sitting thinking how to broach the subject, I felt again that I was on the cusp of revealing something complicated and ominous, the same feeling I had when I walked into the factory next to the RACV.

I told them that someone from Scottish Intelligence had turned informant and that I could find out where they lived. They stared blankly at me and I had an inkling that I had just freaked out two perfectly peaceful people sitting in the park. 'Enjoy yourselves,' I said, and walked away unsatisfied; again I had not got to the root of things. I put my headphones on, and wandered aimlessly through the streets. I drank myself stupid that night, and dossed down in the hostel feeling foetal. Water trickled down inside the hostel walls. The room felt like a dungeon.

I was almost nearly always polite when confronting imagined persecutors such as this, and wonder at schizophrenics with a more angry persona. Yet such was the anger and confusion pent up within me at this stage that I am not surprised that schizophrenic people have killed or hurt people, and I can imagine the kinds of misunderstandings that would have contributed to such tragic events.

 I think I've figured something out here. My mind is fixed in a mode where EVERYTHING that happens in the universe has something to do with me. Everybody is either my friend or my enemy, no neutrals. And more of the latter. There are many people of both sexes that are in love with me, worship me, fear me or hate me.

Here at the apartment I'm being singled out, spied
upon and plotted against. I have told the management
that I will sue for discrimination or, worse yet, retaliate
in some other way. So the police naturally would be
involved. If I'm in public and there's not a crowd,
but there's only one or two people in the area, I have
to hide.

And then there's my family. My parents love me very
much, even too much. But they're my parents after all.
My mother, however, is sexually attracted to me, and
my father is fearful and jealous of me. Which I hate.
I just want to be a son, not a god. As for my brothers,
I'm sure one wants to get me framed for something he
or someone else will do. Or he wants me dead, maybe.
I've always thought that two of my brothers wanted
to kill me as a child, and one damn near almost did.
Broke my neck, nearly.

And I have things in my head, knowledge and beliefs,
that can get me in a lot of trouble with the American
government, military, media/corporate elite, etc. They
may be aware that I know of their plan to Americanize
the whole world, i.e. to make them all white, suburban,
middle-class, English-speaking and Protestant. They
have to raise up more and more boy bands and build
more and more McDonaldses for the invisible czars.
And the rest of the world is planning on how they're
going to fight this off.

It's all because I'm some sort of prophet. Not a Christ,
but a John the Baptist. There will one day be a war in
the area around Jerusalem between the Christians and
the Muslims and I will be caught in the middle with a
group of followers of a new religion, where the other

faiths of the world are united (kinda like the Baha'i faith), and there I will be martyred. Christianity and Islam will effectively destroy each other, and at least one billion will perish in WWIII. The Pope will see his Catholic Church collapse around him and will end up exiled to Axum, Ethiopia for a time.

But my spirit will guide the darkened, desperate world slowly to an era of spiritual peace. Like the Age of Aquarius they used to talk about.

There are forces among the djinn (a term I use for the 'invisible people', spiritual beings that roam the earth; of course taken from Islamic belief), and probably from flesh, blood and bone people, to turn me into a monster. They want me to commit a couple of murders, bomb a few buildings, stalk and rape some women (and a few men). And now I've noticed I don't make much sense to myself anymore. I have to do something. I suddenly wish I had died in infancy so that I didn't have to disrupt the balance of nature with my loudest thoughts. I can't kill myself because I was told it would be impossible. In fact, the day of my death has already been set in stone at Armageddon. I really am the most dangerous person you will probably ever meet.

SAME MIND-SET, DIFFERENT HORIZONS

The time had come for our Kontiki tour around Europe. Ang by this stage was well aware of how I could react to different situations and she was very accommodating. She told me in London that it definitely sounded like schizophrenia. I didn't really agree, though I could see that if my delusions were not real then I was a whole lot better off. Yet I always slipped back into false beliefs.

The European trip was fantastic: I had a great time, although there was many an incident tinged with madness. I remember at one stage announcing to a group of people on the bus, 'A bus-load of wankers is nothing . . . if you and the organisers are serious about the conspiracy, you will be taking it to the mass media'. At this stage I was very wary of everyone, but made a great effort to be sociable and friendly, while skating over my delusions, an ear out here, a suspicion there.

During the trip I began a passionate holiday romance with a woman from Western Australia by the name of Kylie. We would tent up together and spend time in exotic cities together, enjoying gondola rides and amazing galleries, lots of beer drinking and intimate nights. As our physical intimacy grew, so I let her see the workings of my mind day by day.

One night in Germany I went for a long walk before bedtime. I said I would be back soon and walked out of the caravan park and into the streets, taking in German suburbia. As I walked, the screams that I used to hear from my bedroom window back in Australia started to emerge and the more I took notice of them, the louder they became. As I walked and listened, a streetlight that I was walking under suddenly went out, leaving me in the dark. The other streetlights anthropomorphised. It was as if I did not exist any more. I could imagine reality opening up and me stepping into some sort of porthole.

UNEXPECTED

I wandered around for hours. At one stage I got lost and had to use my hunches to get back to where I came from. I walked back into the park, and unzipped the tent. 'Where did you go?' asked Kylie, amazed. Without really wanting to, I told her about the screams coming from all over the neighbourhood, and said that the streetlight that went off near me was a sign full of meaning. I spoke for a few minutes, reliving my walk.What happened next was unexpected: she burst into tears.

We were lying down. She came closer and hugged me, I told her not to worry, I was all right. She confided in me that Ang had warned her of my symptoms, and she told me she was pretty sure I had schizophrenia. As fate would have it, she was a psychiatric nurse, and she told me she had heard it all before, voices, streetlights and so on. She was sobbing, and all I could do was say, 'It will be all right.' this was not the first time my delusional personality had driven someone to tears, yet I really did think everything would be all right.

I was not so much concerned about my mental state – my illness had manifested so slowly I had not noticed its appearance – as worried that I was upsetting people.

When we saw each other off at the airport, we promised each other we would get together again, that I would work in Western Australia in the mines, save up some cash and be back overseas, that this was special, more than just a holiday romance. Back in Australia, some months after our trip had ended, I rang her. It turned out she was engaged the whole time and she was just having a last holiday fling before commitment. In honesty, it didn't matter. I'd enjoyed our time together, and I then didn't feel as bad about fooling with another bloke who was on the tour.

MURPHY'S LAW FOR THE PSYCHOTIC

It was the end of the tour. Ang and I drank a good part of two bottles of Baileys on the ferry back to Dover. I remember it as a good time.

We got off the ferry, back onto the bus and were advised not to apply for working visas on the way through, as they took too long to process and we were already running late, but I applied anyway.

The other people were already on the bus and my visa was still being processed. I was getting itchy because I had already made the bus late numerous times through Europe. The tour manager came up and asked what the problem was, so I confessed that I'd applied for the visa. She rolled her eyes when a person in a uniform came over to speak to me.

'Richard McLean? Can I have a word with you please?'

He told me that I could not apply for a working visa then, and that it would not be granted. He told me that the laws had changed, that you had to apply for your working visa from your country of origin before you got there. I asked when the laws changed. 'Today,' was the unfortunate reply.

There was not much more to say, and I turned on my heel to join the others. He put a hand on my shoulder to stop me. Because he knew I intended to work and could not get my visa, he was not going to let me back into England. In fact, he had me booked back on a ferry to Amsterdam in twenty minutes. The tour organiser pleaded for me but to no avail. Ripping up my visa application was futile too. He said he would see what we could do.

LOCKED UP

Twenty minutes later I was in a room about four by four metres thinking, 'How did I get here?' There were a couple of plastic moulded seats and a small counter, and as I was led in there I heard the definite sound of the door being locked. A few minutes passed and a rough-looking man about thirty years old was taken to the room and told to sit down. I overheard the conversation between the officers and this bloke, and it appeared he was a drug dealer. They asked him if he had ever been to England before, and he denied he ever had. He got a 'Wait here' response.

During the next half-hour he confided in me that he had been in London numerous times before and had been smuggling drugs for years. I was unimpressed. If he was a criminal, then he was not a very good one. The fluorescent lights were surreal, and for a while I forgot my backpacks were on a bus en route to London, and was intrigued by the odd situation I'd found myself in. In the back of my mind was the idea that ASIO had consulted British Intelligence, and for a moment I saw another opportunity to crack the conspirer's facade.

The officers came back after about another half-hour and laid on the table before the drug dealer surveillance pictures taken of him, a copy of his passport, and the addresses that he had stayed at over preceding years. He was still adamant that he had never been to London.

I thought I might be being set up with this feeble character, and I decided right there and then that if I were asked to report anything he had said, I would come clean. I even thought of telling the officers outright but did not want to get involved in anything that could delay my re-entry to the UK.

I had a plane booked back to Greece in three days, and it was decided that if I was definitely on it, and I stayed at the same address for the duration of the time I was in London, they would allow me into England. They led me down corridors and out past barbed-wire tipped fences, to the area where the bus was parked.

WARM FUZZIES

It was a pleasant surprise to find that the group were still there after an hour and a half. Apparently the bus driver and tour guide wanted to leave me behind, saying they were late for their drop-off point, but the 'back of the bus' crew had staged a protest, saying that if I wasn't on the bus then they were not going either. There were cheers when I returned, and it made me feel warm that they had waited for me.

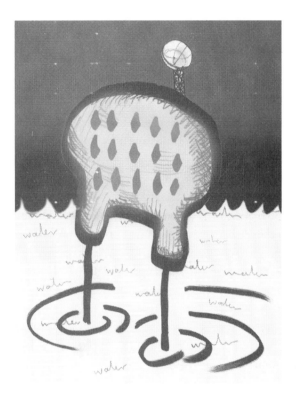

CAPACITOR

The capacitor rendered here as a building is submerged in water and therefore will not work. The people who occupy this building have to look for salvation via the satellite dish – a reflection of helplessness, perhaps.

COMING HOME

Ang and I met up with Kirsten while we were in Greece. We spent a week in Athens and three in the Greek islands, ending up in Turkey near destitute – I had to phone to ask Mum for a cash transfer. Our four-month sojourn was over: I was sad I would not be travelling any more, but happy to see my family and friends again. I felt quite tired yet refreshed when I walked through the gates, and again Mum cried when I came through the door, as all good mums do.

Mum and Dad were surely worried about me. After I had been overseas for a while, one of the first postcards I sent was addressed to our family dog, telling of lots of different smells and parks and things. It was meant to be a joke, but I don't think they got it.

MORE OF THE SAME

After the sharing of photos and experiences, and the joke of 'been there' whenever something European came up on TV, it took only a few weeks to slip right back into my delusional ideas. It reminded me of a school reunion, all the past hierarchies are suddenly back in place exactly as they were when you left.

four
Realisations

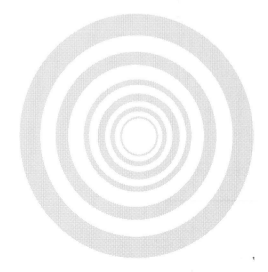

THREE PEOPLE, ONE PERSON
This is a recent image, reflecting the many personas that make up an individual from infant to adult, and influence of anima and animus (Jungian male and female elements) in our being. It may also be a kind of mourning for the person you were who was lost when circumstances changed.

I had been back about a month, listening to the familiar screams outside my window of a night and finding subjective meaning in common conversation. When a friend, Steve, offered me a room at his new rental place in Mordialloc for a couple of weeks, I saw a chance of respite and gladly accepted. After I had been there for that time he offered me the room at fifty bucks a week rent, long-term.

The day I left home, I had my stereo with me, shoved into the boot of Steve's car, and as we were driving off, Dad said, 'Keep in touch.' I guess he knew before I did that I was going to stay for a while. Dad was well aware of my passion for music, and knew that if I had the stereo, I was home and happy.

There was a lady next door who I thought was acting out a conspiratorial part. She was a friendly person by day, yet she had three or four guys on the go at any one point, and often had yelling matches late into the night. Plates were thrown, and the most abrupt language I had ever heard from someone so charming, so friendly during the day.

Our residences were joined by a wall, hence a lot of the time you could hear what was going on. I had let on to Steve that I thought she was giving me secret messages through the wall, and that I had to listen to clues. As comedy would have it, I even tried listening through the wall with a glass, à la Maxwell Smart. Steve accepted these eccentricities and went on playing Super Mario Brothers. I was still conversational enough to be able to carry out day-to-day stuff with Steve. Again, anything I said was just from trippy Richie.

RAMBLINGS

One night I write down my perceptions of messages through the wall in an effort to sort them out. I found the book it was written in recently.

Eurology

Because fuckin' attitude
Gone for an hour
Type school
Could be liking it
(techno goes up)
You getting FEEDBACK?
knows that video
(techno stops)
What about your girlfriend?
had his baby
had his children
(then TV makes noise)
(The video fast forwards of its own accord)
(TV volume is turned down)
(noise in street)
I don't understand you
Send him to the doctors
Why Bother

Why don't do anything
He's a cunt
The thing is . . . Tuesday
Abortion
(cough) Murder
Listen to me, please
If I die that person would want me
Not bad but spare me not
Abort me
Life is an accident
Is that bad or what?
I feel like saying to you You're a cunt, murderer
Shouldn't happen
Going to be miserable for it
The rest of my life knowing I murdered someone
With no one to talk to ...
(video fast forwards by itself again)
November 19
Can't you understand
It'll do
(Dave letterman interruption)
On the streets tomorrow
There's a car outside, it stopped in the kitchen
Tripping you out yet?
I know ... You're only one metre away, do you smell a rat?
Goodbye, it's a run ...
Singled out, its all a blur

It has made me sad typing the above.

FOOLING AROUND

Steve's fiancée Kirsten had a friend, Kath, who would come and stay at weekends. We would invariably get drunk and go spend ten bucks on the pokies. Some weeks we would win and get more trashed, some weeks we would just stay at home and drink goonie juice. I was on with Kath as a matter of convenience, really. Going to sleep, I would ask her if she heard the voices outside. She said she didn't know what I was talking about. As far as I knew, she was quite unaware of my mental state. I had a sneaking suspicion she was lying.

I had on a meditation CD that I had bought a few years earlier called 'Amazonian Forest' or some such New Age title. The first time I meditated to it I was quite relaxed until I heard some noises like howler monkeys being hunted down, which, obviously, were not conducive to relaxation.

I had not listened to it for ages and decided to put it on really low one Friday night. Kath was up having bongs with a mate in the lounge. When she came to bed, the CD was still playing, unbeknown to her. We started chatting and I was talking about the voices to her. She was really stoned and seemed taken in by the lucidity of our conversation. I suspected Kath was in on some sort of conspiracy – often my thoughts would get looser and more psychotic at night time.

Then I did something that will surely see me in purgatory.

It was quite a still night, and the CD was playing really low, and I suggested to Kath that even though there was not much sound, she was suddenly going to hear crickets. After a few minutes, she exclaimed, 'Oh my God, I really can hear crickets.' She was a little freaked by this and she was stoned, so it spun her out even more.

I went on a bit of a rant about how reality is only a facade, that there were many dubious forces at stake in everyday life, and if she let herself be open to the possibility, she too would perceive what I had to deal with day-to-day. Listen carefully, Kath, lift the facade, Kath. Enter the gibbons.

Well, Kath freaked out on hearing these wild animals, holding me tight and saying she was scared, which I'm sure she was in this stoned state. It's something that I wanted to orchestrate for another person, the way that I felt the voices and various stimuli had been orchestrated for me. However, I felt too guilty not to tell her, and got a punch in the chest when I told her it was only a CD. It made me realise that if someone did hear voices such as this, then there was an appropriate reaction, and that I had endured it for God knows how long and had a somewhat different response.

It spawned a moment of clarity that my whole perception was a little warped. I spoke to Steve about it the next day.

'YEAH, YOU NEED HELP, MAL'

I had confided my delusions a few times to Steve – Steve, there are cameras in the house, microphones hidden in the walls, spies monitoring us closely – but up till now he had always taken them with a grain of salt. 'Yeah, I think you should go and see someone, Mal,' Steve would say. He always called me Mal. He was clearly being helpful. 'What can it hurt?' I thought.

ATTEMPT ONE

I went to the medical clinic in Mordialloc and waited to see a doctor. I registered pastel decor, a ratty small palm tree and a few weary-looking people. When my name was called and I went into the small room with the doctor, there were mysterious knocks on the wall next to where I was sitting. I had the sneaking conviction that the conversation was being recorded; that the conspirators were letting me know that they knew I was in there.

'How can I help you?' the doctor asked. Throwing caution and paranoia to the wind, I told him of the reason for the knocks on the wall. I was quite fluent and spoke confidently, a thing I had learnt to do to mask my inner chaos.

'You mean to tell me those knocks have a reason?' he asked. He seemed surprised I would tell him in such a calm manner about the knocks. He was trying to get a grip on what I was saying. No, I said. When I spoke about it out loud, it seemed ridiculous. I told him some of the other things I was experiencing, and he suggested after talking to me for a few minutes that I try to keep regular sleeping patterns.

He was friendly but I got the impression that he was leading me away from the story I wanted to tell him. I took this as confirmation that the conspiracy had liaised with the doctor, that he thought I deserved to be punished. He knew damn well what was going on. The fact that he hadn't questioned theories that even I thought were ridiculous proved it.

I didn't know then that a lot of doctors were not that well versed in psychiatry – I didn't even know the difference between psychology and psychiatry at that point. This doctor saw a person who was a little odd maybe, but generally well-mannered, and he sent me on my way. I felt confused. I had had enough feedback to make me think there really was something wrong with my mind, but underneath was an unshakable conviction that there really was something vast and threatening out there. I chose to put the whole episode to the back of my mind. Stuff doctors.

 I too have thoughts which are not my own, telling me to hurt myself (castration and at the moment to destroy my hearing so then I can't hear them any more???) and I am also paranoid and feel that I must hide this. I have started believing that my therapist is studying me/recording me – that she is up to something which I can't understand – but on one level realize this can't be true so I must hide this from her and thereby not resolving the problem? (does that make sense?)

NEW STUDENT

While I was away, Mum had looked at a few courses for me to do, and as soon as I was back I found myself at an interview for computer art and design. The course offered animation, which I had always been interested in. They accepted me on the spot and I was happy to get back into studying mode again. The workforce seemed too stressful, but I liked being a student and being exposed to different things.

Starting a new course, I was generally conversational yet suspicious. People probably thought I was just a little shy. I showed a fellow student my sketchbook. She made a comment along the lines of 'Wow, you must have a lot on your mind.' I seemed to speak well one on one, but in group situations I found it hard to follow conversation, and always read extra meanings aimed at me. I still sometimes feel like this. I chose to keep to myself.

I just found this website. I am looking for people who don't judge me. That's hard to ask since I judge myself constantly. I live in a place with others like me, yet so different. I am starting school again, but I need some encouragement. The last time I was in school I had to drop out because I tried to kill myself which I feel bad

about trying. But I know if I drop out again I will
disappoint my family and myself. I have not had any
bad auditory hallucinations for a while. Everyone in my
family says to ignore it. I wish it was that easy. Thanks
for listening.

STEVE'S LOUNGE ROOM
This is representative of the sketches I did when I was living with Steve. It's
interesting that an image of such chaos can emerge from simply sitting in the
lounge room watching television. There are familiar themes here, in the flatness
of the image and the old circle, square, triangle of years gone by.

SPEAKER SEARCH

When Steve came home from work, he would play computer
games for a while, perhaps to escape from work. He introduced me to it, and a few weeks later I was absolutely hooked,

and would play it till at least three each morning. Late at night, my hallucinations would subtly appear. When I turned off the Nintendo, I could still hear its lollipop music, and as I went to sleep, I would hear the theme music of Mario Brothers in my ears amongst the screams. It had me on all fours looking for speakers.

One night, I was looking up the chimney for cameras and microphones when some ash fell from the chimney into the fireplace, hinting at something clandestine. I could not see anything there, yet was totally convinced that something or someone was up there. I placed a piece of paper in the fireplace to catch any fresh evidence that might fall.

I attributed to the conspiracy such intelligence and stealth that I knew I would not be able to catch them out. Yet I also held to the idea that the conspiracy was so huge that someone, somewhere would slip up, and then I might be able to sue them in some way for persecuting me. I wanted proof, I wanted the mass media, I wanted to make the voices real and recordable. I was desperately searching for tangibility in what seemed an anchorless fight.

THE SNOW

Steve, Kirsten, Kath and I and a few others ventured up to the snow for the day. The others were having a great day but I heard voices all the way there and was generally having a bad time to the tune of 'Fuck you stupid' and 'You're dead.' At one point I was giggling at the ridiculousness of it all, but ended up huddled in a foetal position, shivering, in the back of the car while the others went skiing and tobogganing. All I wanted was to escape my own brain. I had definitely lost my zest, my passion, my thirst for experience. To be without stimuli would be refreshing.

At the end of the day the others got into the car, and as always, I talked enough to project the usual slightly eccentric, yet more or less normal Rich – maybe. In fact, I really had no idea of what they all thought at this point. It wasn't on my agenda to find out.

All the way home I heard Steve making the most crushing comments to me from the driver's seat. I tried to see his mouth in the rear-vision mirror, to catch him out when he said these things to me, but I couldn't see properly. I asked him politely to repeat himself a few times, he responded that he had not said anything. I did not believe him. Same old same old.

I politely say, 'I have to go home first, thanks, Steve, to my parents' house'. He obliges and when I get out of the car I let my guard down. I say, 'Fuck you'.

At this point Steve had had enough of my unpredictable behaviour and eccentricities. Astounded, he snapped, 'Fuck you, Mal!' and stormed off in the car back to Mordialloc. The girls were, I suppose, a little surprised by the whole incident.

I asked my dad to drive me to Mordialloc. I didn't say much on the way. When I got back there, all my stuff was packed and I was asked to move out.

GET HELP!

I realised this was serious and decided to open up to Steve. I apologised for being unreasonable and told him that I heard people in the car voicing various insults and threats. Again, I was driven to the point of saying feebly, 'I think I should see someone about this'. But even as I said it, I wasn't convinced I should.

Steve totally agreed and we talked it over. It was decided I could stay if I sought help. I went to sleep with the screaming in my ears, and the challenge of finding someone who might have an understanding of what was happening and know how to solve it. I was not enthralled by the challenge. I still doubted anything was wrong.

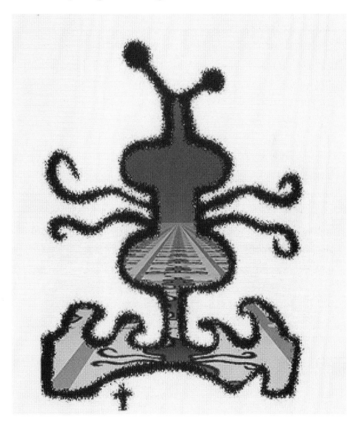

GRAPHIC SYMBOL

At this time I was trying to extract the absolute essence of an idea and represent it in the simplest way possible. Here is a resistor being inundated with water. There are other thematic elements (suggested subliminally) from lions to dead fish, indicating that the attempt to resolve and simplify my thoughts hasn't entirely worked. The perspective reflects a fantasy I still have sometimes of a door opening onto a different dimension – probably a metaphor for exploration of new areas.

five

Doctors and Drugs

FINGERS DO THE WALKING

A few days later I flicked through the Yellow Pages, looking under 'Psychologist', and found one that was close to where I lived. I called up and said, 'I'd like to make an appointment, please'. The receptionist asked if I had a referral, and I said I didn't. I didn't really know what she meant. She explained.

A day later I was back in the doctor's pastel-coloured office in Mordialloc, with the unwatered, sick-looking palm tree, thinking this is too much of a déjà vu. I got the doctor that I saw before and I asked him outright for a referral to a psychologist. I didn't go into any detail, only telling him it was a matter of life and death. Looking back, that could have been true.

> I have been thinking of getting help for the last couple of weeks. I have no clue on how to do so. I have hardly any money. I mow a couple of yards for food and cigs. So I am not able to pay for an appointment. I have looked in the phone book and I can only find clinics that charge

money. The last time I went to a dr. it was $85 an appointment. I had a job with insurance luckily back then. That was early 1999. I haven't worked since then or been to a dr. I can't go to my parents or relatives. I have $15 in my pocket. I am living in the basement underground, sleep most of the day. Everyone asks me why don't you talk. My family despises me. The only reason they let me come back home was because I got arrested earlier this year. I feel like they make me stay in the basement so I won't embarrass them. Have to be popular, you know, no weirdos here. This summer they had some people over for a cookout. I went up to use the bathroom and everyone was at the table eating. Since they saw me they had to introduce me. This one lady said we have never met him, but they knew my brother and sister for many years. They didn't even know they had another son. I can't stand having the light on. Being in the basement it is really dark. The basement is better than my old room, inside the furnace room. I loved it, but it was dark and noises abounded.

Everybody else got a room when we moved seven years ago. I got a damn furnace room. And I am the oldest. It didn't bother me then because I didn't have to see anybody. When I was in the hospital they didn't even tell me what was wrong with me.

What do I do? I have a hard time communicating with anyone. Even in past appointments I have not told the dr. most of the things I experience for fear. I try but the words don't come out. I would tell my parents but they just tell me to snap out of it and get a job. Sometimes I feel I have to hurt somebody or hurt myself to get

help. I have a cat and a bird so that is out of the
question. If not for them I probably wouldn't be here.
I am in a lonely and frightening place and I can't get
out. I know I need to take the first step but I don't know
how. Sorry for rambling, but I am confused and scared.
HOW DO I GET HELP?

'GIVE ME A HAND WITH THIS LADDER'

In the weeks before the appointment with the psychologist, I
was quite delusional. I could hear the strangest sounds, like
people in agony, emanating from the roof above my bedroom
as I tried to go to sleep.

MORDIALLOC LANDSCAPE
Making images was often very therapeutic for me; I would feel exultant
at completing even simple sketches like this one. Making marks with a
black oil stick as I did in this picture seemed at once to liberate esoteric
ideas and to ground me.

I had had enough of these voices from the roof and when Steve got home the next day he caught me on a chair trying to look up through the manhole in the roof. I was looking for speakers and the cameras that were tracking my position, but I told Steve I suspected there were rats in the roof and I was just checking for droppings.

He helped me with the ladder, and I climbed halfway up into the roof. In the back of my mind I felt I was being ridiculous, but I still believed with absolute conviction that something was going on. I saw a few wires and a lot of dust, and it turned out we did have rats, judging by the droppings, but no cameras, much to my disappointment.

You can't imagine my confusion when I heard voices emanating from inside the roof again that night.

DIANA THINKS I'M PSYCHO

I ran into Diana at the supermarket. We got along well and I was looking at her as a potential girlfriend. We cooked each other meals and had endless things to talk about. I rode my bike to her house one night about a week later, and knocked on the door. No one was home.

I had brought my camera with me to take photos of personalised numberplates that I believed were revealed to me as a form of persecution. In my room I had endless pieces of paper with numberplates written on them in code. I had still not cracked their message. Every time a new one appeared, I thought I was getting closer. I am forever on the verge of finding the secrets of the universe, yet they never manifest.

On my way home, the police flashed their lights at me – I think now for not having a helmet – and in a blind panic I tried to outrun them. Sirens screaming after me, I sped down a side street and rode as best I could along a beach until the sand slowed me to a halt. I collapsed on the ground, puffing. For some reason, I decided to take a picture of my feet. Somehow, I wanted to remember what I was going through.

When the cops had gone, I went back to Diana's place. There were still no lights on, and I looked in the front window to see if she was there.

Weeks later I heard from Karen that Diana thought I was nuts and had come around several times to peer in her windows. I was outraged. Years later I accepted her apology and moved into a house with her that was going to be demolished. One day Diana decided she didn't like a wall and took to it with a saw and an axe. Another story . . .

The appointment with the psychologist was on a street called High Street. The psychologist asked, 'How can I help?' I decided at this point that I had had enough of my brain, and in a moment of clarity told her about speakers, car number-plates, Rex Hunt talking to me from the TV and Australian bands writing songs about me, among other things. I felt lucid and spoke with detachment. I noticed a box of tissues next to me in the comfortable chair in which I was sitting, reflecting that probably many people came in here, vented their problems and cried. I couldn't remember the last time I had cried.

The meeting went for about twenty minutes, and she explained that I needed to see another doctor and there was a simple course of medication that I could take. She said mine was a very common experience and I should see the doctor that she had referred me to. She also explained that as a psychologist, she could not prescribe the medication.

I saw it as another wasted effort. As I drove home with a bill for seventy bucks I was wholly dissatisfied. I wasn't getting anywhere, people were taking me for a ride, shuffling me here, sending me there. On the way home I saw a couple of numberplates, and read them as anagrams of sentences that told me I was being tracked. Same old same old.

I had yet to solidify my experiences into definitions that would make sense of my existence.

✉*!* I always pictured it as interconnecting rooms with long hallways, that would slowly keep growing like a tree's roots, but then slowly turn back in on itself and finally implode . . . but now I can barely remember what it looked like . . .

ENDURING THE WEEKS

I filed away the referral letter to the psychiatrist, Dr X, and didn't give it much further thought. As far as I was concerned, it was clear that people were trying to make me think I was going mad by planting numberplates, sending messages via TV and radio, and spying on me whenever I was out and about. People who tried to tell me I showed symptoms of schizophrenia seemed to me to be plotting to delude and destabilise me.

On the other hand, if I found a book on psychology or psychiatry in an op shop I would always buy it. I'm sure that countless people affected by schizophrenia and similar illnesses do not seek help because they believe they are not sick and the people around them don't recognise the symptoms.

Dad generously bought me an old car, a Gemini, that I could drive around in. It was a bit of a bomb, but I loved it and it gave me the freedom to drop back to my parents' house, which I did often. I applied for graphics jobs online, and faxed résumés from the home computer. It's hard to get a foot in with no experience.

I liked my new TAFE course and the people were generally friendly. One guy, though, I was suspicious of. His name was Roman, and he had been sent to track my moves in this new environment, I was sure of it.

One day I sat opposite him and heard voices, as if from a small radio or CB, emanating from his bag. It was confirmed – he was a spy.

I calmly asked him, 'Do you have a radio in your bag?' He replied negatively, somewhat disconcerted by the odd nature of my question. I often wonder what a difference it would have made if I had been the kind of person who says whatever they think out loud. I sat and listened to the voices coming from his bag for a while. As always with such voices, they started whenever I looked away, and when I looked at the source, they would stop.

Sitting in class that day, I thought, 'I can't handle this any more.' I went outside and smoked a few cigarettes. In a moment of clarity, I was convinced that something was wrong with my mind. That night I decided to talk to Steve about it – again.

I told him about the voices coming from the bag, among other things. It was hard to have a conversation about my surreal experiences; more often than not, I would push them to the back of my mind when the opportunity to express them arose. I was beginning to realise how ridiculous this was, the voices and delusions dominating my thoughts.

I wrapped up by saying, more rethinking an affirmation than asking a question, 'Do you think I should see that doctor?' Steve wholeheartedly agreed and said it couldn't hurt just to see what they said. I decided then and there I should go and see this doctor, although it seemed such a chore, and all I wanted to do was to forget about my mind-set, not have to talk about it and re-live it. It was a huge challenge I was setting for myself. If you're familiar with people who are mentally ill, you will know the challenge to get them to see someone.

THE APPOINTMENT

I drove to a community centre in suburban Melbourne and upon entering, the receptionist told me to take a seat. There was a wide range of services available at the centre, and I reflected that I was here to see the psychiatrist, but would rather see a dentist.

The receptionist called me over again. She told me there would be a wait to see Dr X, but there was no reason for this other than that he was busy with another client. I said, 'No worries' and sat down again. Moments later it occurred to me that she was over-explaining so that I would not be suspicious of why I was waiting.

I was staring into space when Dr X emerged with his last patient. I was curious to see the guy, about 25 years old, thin, shabbily dressed, mumbling 'Thank you' and shuffling out the door. 'Richard McLean?' 'Yes.' I went in. I didn't really want to be there. I was going to get this over with quick smart.

'Sit down,' he said, 'be with you in a minute'.

I sat there, looking at the back of his head. He had on a Jewish cap. He was a big fellow with glasses and a thick Jewish beard. The moment I thought 'What is the Jewish stance on androgynous sexuality, art, religion, etc?' I heard his voice mumbling from around the back of his head.

'Ahh, we've got you now, cunt.'

I was in two minds: one harboured all the fierce energy, the guilt, sadness, hallucinations and delusions, the confusion that my brain had been putting on me for the last few years, and one wanted to tell this amalgam of the last few years where to fuck off.

I was instantly stoic again. I thought there might be bugs located in yet another pastel-coloured office with a cheesy fern in the corner. I had thought many times that if I was going to see a doctor, then I would want it to be outside in a park or something, so no one could bug us. I flirted with the idea of telling him to come outside, then reneged, pushing the idea to the back of my mind.

WHAT BRINGS YOU HERE?

Dr X turned to face me. 'What brings you here?' he asked. In tense situations, I sometimes resort to terseness. In response to his question, I replied, 'I'm fucked.' It was a huge effort, but strangely a relief to say it.

He asked me to elaborate. I thought, 'It's now or never,' and told him of the things I'd been going through, in a stark and retrospective way. I felt emotionally flat, and talking about my experiences and ideas out loud made them seem ridiculous. It was a leap of faith to confide in him, I had in mind he was the enemy. In the back of my mind I thought the meeting served two purposes: to talk to him honestly, and to show the conspirers what pain they were causing – it might make them call the whole thing off. I thought he might confide in me either way.

ARE YOU HAPPY?

He told me of a simple medication that I could take to end all these problems. He knew I was not buying any of it and he knew all too well that deep down I thought he was the enemy.

He asked me how I felt in my younger teenage years, and said I could achieve this happiness again if I co-operated in taking a course of medication. It was a simple process of taking a small dose then increasing it to a beneficial level where there were not too many side effects.

His professionalism was impeccable, and without that meeting, I do not know where I would be now.

He gave a solid argument that the medication would help, but said that it was my choice to take it or not. He explained the pros and cons, and left the ball in my court. I took the prescription. He wanted to see me the next week. Fighting every instinct, I agreed. I thought, 'I have nothing left to lose.'

 I'm new to the site. I guess I seeked out the site to see if there is anyone else out there going through what I am. My husband of 11 years was diagnosed 2 years ago with Schizophrenia. I was able to force him into a hospital to get him help twice in that 2 year period. He now knows how to beat the system. He is not violent, so I can't, by law, commit him to get help anymore. #1 he refuses that he has a problem and, therefore he refuses to take his meds. He believes people around him, such as his brother, mom, dad and myself are the devil. He thinks we hypnotize him and other people to get them 'under our power'. I have moved out as of May of this year. I am afraid of him because of the way he talks, not because he has actually hurt me. He will say things like 'I'll get you back someday', 'You will all pay for what you have done', etc. We have been going to a counselor and nothing will seem to work. The counselor tried to make him realize that he has an imbalance that is causing him to think of things that are not actually happening, but all he does is laugh at him. We got no where. Legally, I can't do anything to force medication on him. At this point, I feel I have no other choice but divorce. We also have 2 children together, so that is very hard. I guess I just take one day at time.

IT WILL MAKE YOU GROW BREASTS

I got home that night, stressed by the day's events. Stress is one of the precursors to a psychosis and can bring on an episode if the person is susceptible. In my case I had the usual youthful angst plus ideas due to my delusions to cope with.

Immediately after going to the chemist to pick up the script, I went home to Mordialloc. I opened the box. The blue pills contained an antipsychotic called Stelazine.

I read the small print on the leaflet that came with the box. *This medication may cause drowsiness and may increase the effects of alcohol. If affected, do not drive a motor vehicle or operate machinery.* It warned of the most bizarre side effects, such as possible growth of breasts in males and females, and even lactation. 'How did I get myself into this situation?' I snapped back to delusion shortly after. In my mind, the idea was concrete that there was still a conspiracy, that everyone I knew was either in on it or being dragged down with me.

ONE PILL HAPPY, TEN PILLS VERY HAPPY

I believed the drugs I had been given were anti-depressants. I desperately wanted to be happy, I desperately wanted to be sane. My delusional and irresponsible mind came up with a naive formula: one pill, happy; ten pills, very happy.

Disregarding what the packet said, I washed down about ten pills with a swig of beer. I stopped and thought how ridiculous I felt. But what if these pills could make me sane? I washed down a few more.

I went to sleep with the voices outside saying hideous things, all related to the stressful day I had just had, the meeting with the doctor, and the pills. I turned the stereo up, and they became louder and more aggressive, so I turned it down to listen . . . nothing. I turned it back up again and they were back. I had little faith in the drugs. I had little faith in anyone or anything.

 I try so hard, everything I do is useless. People expect more out of me than I can give. The voices are coming more often now. I'm getting depressed again. I was looking so good, so normal and now I'm back to being psychotic. I'm really scared. I know how schizophrenia works (from research and living with it) and I know what's going to happen to me once I'm off my meds since its beginning to happen to me already.
It's such a hard fight and I don't know how much more I can take. I'm not suicidal. Everyone where I live says I'm looking better, healthier and that kind of stuff but

> they're wrong. I am just putting on an act when I look
> good on the outside. On the inside I'm really messed up.
> Strangers are trying to poison me again. I'm constantly
> living in a nightmare where I can never wake up. I'm
> ugly fat stupid and can't do anything right anymore. I'm
> a puppet, I'm a slave since I have thought monsters,
> powerful forces (even though they're really nice
> masters to me) and demons controlling me. I used to be
> such a sweet beautiful innocent child and now that
> poor little girl is dead and in her place is a psychotic
> person. I'm such a failure. Who would want me as a
> girlfriend? I daydream about having a husband and kids
> but that's all just a dream. I don't think it could ever
> become a reality. My future is ruined, I'm ruined.

I was late for school that day. In class, I rocked back and forward on my chair so much so that it was commented on by a
few people. Every fifteen minutes I would have to get up and
take a walk, yet by the afternoon I was so tired I fell asleep on
a chair outside my classroom. One of the staff walked past
with a guest of the school as I woke up. 'One of our sleeping
babies,' she said.

THE NEXT APPOINTMENT

I went to my follow-up appointment with Dr X. By this time I
had decided to take the medication in the right dose.

I sat in the waiting room in his private practice and could
hear voices talking from the consulting room. I could not fight
the impulse to eavesdrop on what was being said in the next
room, although the sound was muffled

I sat down and he began asking me all sorts of questions,
from how often I had sex to my relationship with my family,

what I did for school and the like. I found it hard to look at him because, very oddly I thought, and still do, he had an index finger down his throat to the top knuckle, and only took it out to ask questions. I thought the man was a freak and to this day I am wary of people like him fucking with my mind.

Going back week after week, then every two weeks, then every month, I was still astounded at the way Dr X put his finger down his throat, and wondered if he did it to freak patients out. I have often thought the temptation for a doctor to say, 'Yes, God is speaking through the radio to you,' or something similar would be strong sometimes.

 I have had mistrust of my psychiatrist – this is very difficult because she/he is the one person who can help you. I started to think that he was in on the whole conspiracy against me. It was awful, 'cause really he's a sweety. I have also thought that my psychiatrist was recording me, or that people were listening in to our conversations. I told him that I was having these thoughts and it helps to know that he knows somehow.

I was aware that any doctor I saw might not be the ideal, and might not agree with my views on sex, religion and things of a metaphysical nature. I tried to please my doctor and impress him with how well I was doing by speaking rather distantly of my continuing delusions. In retrospect, I realise I really should have dropped to the floor and wailed about how messed-up I was. It probably would have been a whole lot more beneficial in those first sessions.

 I went to my psych yesterday because he was worried about me. When I went in there I felt like I was going to explode. I haven't been sleeping, my head is driving me insane and I'm scared of everyone around me and of myself. I feel like I have been taken over by my demons again.

It was a really full-on conversation. I spent the first half hour trying to convince him that I was fine and that everything was going well. Big mistake. He didn't believe me and got angry at me. Then I got angry and blurted out all this stuff that I have been trying so hard to hide. Not because I didn't trust him but because I know that other people listen to everything that I say and the more I say the closer they are to catching me. Everything seems to be spinning out of control. I have tried so hard to be normal, to ignore all the screaming

PORTRAIT
This image was very quickly made with a scanned Stelazine pill and its label. It suggests the feelings I've had of existing within a chemical straitjacket. I wonder if matters of the heart are changed by medication, if it changes who you are in essence.

in my head, but I can't control myself anymore. I think something may be wrong and it scares me. I don't know what I'm going to do or even what's happening to me but it looks as if they are going to send me back to the hospital. I don't think people realise how hard I have to fight to still even be here. I know my doctor really cares and I think he is a genuine person because he has worked so hard to keep me out of hospital. But now they are going to lock me up and I don't know what to do, I just wish my nightmare would be over. I can't live a whole life of this.

six

Recovery

THE JOURNEY BACK

As the weeks passed, I started to trust that Dr X really was trying to help. In the light of my previous delusions, and my ideas of people around me, this was nothing short of miraculous. We increased my medication week by week, as I still had the symptoms, but the delusions bothered me less, as I was not reading new evidence for them into every situation.

I was always very tired, though, and often had to have afternoon naps. I found it hard to get up out of bed in the mornings, and was also experiencing what Stelazine users will know as the 'Stelazine stomps' – a compulsion to jiggle your legs. This was as annoying to me as it was to other people.

DELUSION FADES

In those couple of months of upping my dose, my waking life was a lot more controlled, even though I had side effects. For example, I stopped video-recording TV programs (to collect evidence), because I no longer had faith in the messages. Sure, there were coincidences and things I could have read meaning into, but they didn't manifest in my mind with any sort of solidity. The voices at night seemed to fade away, and

I stopped believing that any random noise was in fact messages meant for me.

I had of course told my parents of my taking medication, Mum casually commented, 'That's nothing!' I am sure she was relieved that we had found some sort of reason for my behaviour, and that my parents had confidence that it would not hold me back. They have continued to support me lovingly; they have and do give me strength. Some people are not as lucky.

Hi everyone. I am worried about my 17-year-old stepdaughter because her behaviour is odd. Let me explain. About a year or so ago she became interested in Eastern religion and now sits Indian-style on the bare floor for an hour or so at a time. She has also become vegetarian and refuses to eat the meals I cook. She states that she won't eat any 'sentient beings'.
I don't understand her logic at all. Fish isn't meat, yet she won't eat it either.
She's paranoid about chemical sprayed on fruit and veggies and will only eat organic.
Also she has some type of obsession with Van Morrison. Last week she went out and spent her whole paycheck on his CDs. Shouldn't she be listening to Britney Spears, Creed and the Backstreet Boys? Do you think she has some sort of father complex?
I think she has some sort of mental illness and think she needs therapy.

(The only reply this imbecile got was 'I think you should just leave her alone'.)

MORE DRUGS

In the weeks that ensued, I began to talk more openly about previous experiences such as waking to find entities in my room, or my theories about time. As I'm now aware of course, those metaphysical obsessions can be a symptom in themselves. The psychiatrist told me to double my meds. I nearly turned around and said religion was delusion en masse, but didn't. So I began to monitor my own medication as I saw fit, only liaising with him on any questions I had to do with my illness. I also began to censor my conversations, and avoided telling him anything that seemed a little wild metaphysically. I only told him things that I felt were relevant to the task at hand.

To combat the stomps, he prescribed another drug called Cogentin, which is mainly used to treat tremors for people with Parkinson's disease. This made me even more drowsy than I already was. At school I would have little naps at my desk while the other students worked around me – I just couldn't stay awake. After a few weeks, I decided I could live with the stomps and stopped the Cogentin treatment.

I later found out that some people who have been on Stelazine for years often develop a syndrome called tardive dyskinesia, causing involuntary movements of the mouth, tongue or face. This also can be treated with Cogentin, with varied results depending on the severity of the syndrome.

I looked up the meds I am on . . . namely Cogentin . . . and found out some horrendous things about it. I am 43 and have been on my current medication for 14 years plus others such as Largactil, Stelazine and Zyprexa. I am coming to the end of my tether . . . lately I have had constantly slurred speech and other reactions . . . I am starting to believe that I have Tardive Dyskinesia (Parkinsonism) . . . I said to my hubby the other nite, well, who is gonna take care of me when I get older with Parkinsonism, I can only look forward to premature admission to an old folks home where they'll just throw away the key & forget about me. I am really really seriously considering coming off all drugs, injections or tablets. And the side-effects tablets aren't much help as far as TD goes, in fact Cogentin can speed my deterioration. I see my psychiatrist in 10 days. This illness has got me beat. Best Wishes to all

There are now newer medications used for schizophrenia and related illnesses that have fewer unwanted side effects.

CHASING MEDICATION

Not long ago, I ran out of medication. I was not concerned; sometimes I had let a few days go by without me getting another script. I was enjoying being much more awake, alert, and actually experiencing laughter of a kind that made my body rush. I joked with friends, I was having a lot of fun and asked them with tongue-in-cheek humor to warn me if I start to go mad in the absence of medication. They didn't worry, they knew I'd get another prescription before I went down that path.

 Please don't discontinue your meds at all, especially if you feel that you are a danger to others. This is so very, very, important. If you feel you have lost something, maybe you could try to see things from a more positive perspective such as this: inside, you feel as though you had a special connection to something out there that

others don't understand, as if you had an insight.
Regardless of whether what you thought was real was
real, the feeling is indisputable. Perhaps you feel
depressed at the thought that this was a fantasy. Well
how about the idea that if in fact there really is more
than meets the eye in this world, then it's worth taking
the time to really appreciate things like the true beauty
of a flower that grows towards the sun, or the way you
feel so good when you laugh at something really funny
or the smell of freshly cut grass and how good the body
feels when it's exhausted but fulfilled after swimming
and alive and buzzing after a run . . . Most people who
are 'normal' don't even appreciate these simple, simple
things, as they are so caught up in work/money/
solutions to problems/materialism/how they are
perceived/pollution/what's going to happen next . . .
the very same stressful things that make
schizophrenics feel particularly stressed. Ultimately,
we are all the same, though perhaps under different
circumstances. You might find that taking the time to
find the extraordinary beauty (goodness and positive
energy), the surrealism and an appreciation in the most
oddly mundane things, quite satisfying. Natural
magical phenomenon that it's so much easier to
take for granted than to ever even notice.

When I run out of meds, I usually just go to any GP, explain
the situation, and receive a new prescription. It is usually five
repeats and lasts me a few months. I went to my local GP to
ask for a script. She coldly replied she didn't even know if I
had schizophrenia and she was unwilling to give me a prescription. I was amazed and angry. Not for the first time,

I wished mental illness was as obvious as a broken leg.

As for my friends and workmates they don't know that
there is anything wrong, as they can't see it. The one
good thing about schiz is that you can't tell who has it.
My parents tell me how can I be ill when I look so
normal. My answer to that is how is a person with
mental illness supposed to look, after all I am still
human and thank god I don't look sick because it makes
it easier to be inconspicuous. The advantage of that is it
makes it easier to overcome the fear of what's going on
inside because I know people can't see I am able to deal
with them and it gets easier and easier. This illness is
a battle and anyone with it is a fighter with the
potential of recovery. The problem is we are our own
worst enemies. You have got to stand up to your fears
to overcome them.

The GP wanted me to get a referral from the psychiatrist
that put me on medication in the first place. I had not seen
him for nearly five years. She seemed to be trying to make
things as difficult as possible. She did, however, give me a
sample pack of the drug, enough for three nights.

A week later, after numerous phone calls and faxes, I made
another appointment with my GP, feeling symptomatic and
disordered through lack of meds. I got a script, went immediately to the chemist and took a double dose. An hour later, the
lethargy hit: it was a familiar feeling, totally unenjoyable, yet I
knew I must start to endure it again or face the consequences.

The medications rob you of feeling, of joy, and taking them
is like ascending the gallows. Accepting that I am better
off with them rushing around my bloodstream, I joke with

friends about taking my 'happy pills', and at the frequent moments of reality-checking with friends ironically ask if they know of any brains going cheap. It is always forced humour, I'm fucking sick of mine.

RENEWING ACQUAINTANCE WITH DOCTOR X

I went to Dr X again. I had not seen him in nearly five years. I had twenty minutes to go through that five years, symptoms, new medications, everything. I wanted to know how I might go about treating residual symptoms, and I wanted to try a new med, as the old one had added 12 kilograms to my weight over the time I had been on it. He suggested Saraquel, and threw me a starter pack, enough for four days. He said to make an appointment in two weeks time to monitor the dose and check that it was working.

'Anything else?' he asked, wrapping up the conversation.

I asked if there was enough medication to last the two weeks. He threw me another box from across the room.

I got home and calculated there would be enough medication to last me eight days. I called immediately and explained this to the secretary; she said he would call me back. He didn't. If the phone did ring I would have felt like saying, 'Oh, Dr X, sorry I was making a mistake – I thought you were someone who gave a shit.'

Nowadays I am relatively well on one of the newer psychotics, Zyprexa, or chemical name Olanzapine – which in turn has its own side effects.

 Do we all know what Zyprexa stands for? Let me repeat myself in case anyone missed it the first time around:

Zaps
Your
Psychosis
Really
EXpands
Ass!

Have you seen the Zyprexa logo? Inside every thin person is a fat person waiting to evolve with the help of Zyprexa!

We who have a mental illness seem to be very attached to those nasty little white pills that are used to make sure we don't slip into the dark abyss of psychosis. I've heard some describe it as a wonderland but for me it definitely wasn't wonderful. Those little tablets sometimes have side effects which make our legs shake, our eyes go up, or our bellies to be stretched like Santa Claus. When we start a new drug we seem to have a special longterm relationship with our pillows. I remember when I first started Olanzapine, 4 years ago. I would get up for lunch, then back to bed. Dinner and a bit of TV then back to bed. A very dull and frustrating experience to say the least.

Maybe someday there will be a cure for illnesses such as schizophrenia and bi-polar disorder. Believe me I would be the first one to sign up if I could. Until then we will keep psychiatrists employed, drug companies making a mint, organisations having their meetings and politicians slashing our budgets. It seems to me quite funny that a little white pill can be the start of such a ruckus.

CHOICE

I believe there is some choice in regard to medication. If you are happy and symptomatic, then why not continue that way. In my case, however, I weighed up the pros of medication as opposed to the cons, and decided that I was happier and more functional with medication. One friend of mine stated that he would rather be dead than to be forced to have monthly injections and weigh thirty kilos more than he had previously. He said his body felt like a rotting vegetable. Nowadays he is free and symptomatic.

I think that when a person has battled an illness for a long period of time, and when medication is added to the mix, they can lose sight of who they were for so many years, the ideas and feelings that identified who they are. It is a shame that people who identify with their illness as a part of themselves cannot afford the luxury of leaving it behind, it's just too damaging to their self-image (something that everyone, especially the mentally ill, fights hard for).

I am very lucky in that I was responsive to medication, and the benefits outweigh the side effects.

When I was first diagnosed, the impact of what 'schizophrenia' meant finally hit me. I wrote a poem to express what I was thinking and feeling. I was horrified, and yet relieved. In the poem I expressed wonder at what would become of me in the years to come. Would I get my sanity back, or was I destined to live a life in and out of the local psychiatric hospital? Would my children remember me fondly as a good mother, or would they have memories of visiting me in the psych ward? Would my husband ever get back the wife he married, or would our relationship evolve into a new caretaker/dependant role? As a diagnosed schizophrenic, was I destined to a life of halfway houses, day programs and mental health coping classes, or would I live out my days at home?

 I'm afraid how my parents will react. My mum will probably tell me to snap out of it and that 'It's just a phase', because she doesn't understand that illnesses can happen to anybody. My dad will go dramatic and then say you can't do this or you can't do that because people are influencing you to act like this. My mum thinks I'm Satanised. How horrible is that? She thinks I have started some weird worship, because he says that I don't talk to anyone and I talk to myself. I can't help it and I can't live with it! My friends don't understand and think I'm emotionally strange or crazy. It's not only destroying my dignity but also my life. I don't know what to do. Please, please help.

REALITY IS BORING

A few months after I began medication many of my symptoms had disappeared. I no longer chased cars to look at numberplates, or tuned into the radio for messages. I began to enjoy radio again. The drawback was that life was less interesting. Instead of feeling that I was always at the centre of something, albeit unpleasant, I found reality enveloped me in greyness and boredom.

 During the past 10 years I made the terrible mistake (twice) of thinking I was well and stopped taking my medication. I got sick again and was hospitalised. I didn't want to think that I had schizophrenia.

> I have to confess that I am not over the shame I feel.
> It's not something I can talk to people about so I feel
> I have a dirty little secret. It affects my relationships
> with women as I can't tell them of the shame I feel.
> I probably seem weak but I really want to be accepted
> by people for what I am (which includes having
> schizophrenia).

It's not that I missed being psychotic; the difference was that I went from being waves on a beach to a particle of sand. Some of my 'messages' were not persecuting, just cryptic, and they provided me with endless stimuli to ponder. In a way I missed it. All the same, I was much happier than I had been for a number of years, and I reflected that had I been born in another age, I could well have been put in Bedlam or burned at the stake.

My doctor said I was lucky in that I responded to treatment very well, and that it took some people a lot longer to respond, while some unfortunate individuals did not respond at all.

My life has become hell. I was diagnosed with schizophrenia earlier this year but have been in and out of hospitals for a few years. My doctor and I have a really good relationship, but he can't help me and admits that he doesn't know what to do.
I am allergic to all the anti-psychotics I have ever been prescribed and now there are none left. I have no hope left. I hate myself, I don't understand what's happening to me and why it's happening to me. I was once intelligent and full of life but have been reduced to live a life that's not worth living. I can't stand it. I don't feel safe on my own but when around others I freak out.

I can't eat, sleep or even think. Does anyone understand what I'm saying? Please, if any one out there does can you offer me some advice or even just a little bit of hope, something that I can hang onto until my doctor figures out a way to help if there's a way to help.

I'M FINE, I DON'T NEED THIS SHIT

Six months later, life was generally stable and happy and one night, I just decided that I was well and didn't need it. I was just about symptom-free and had never felt better.

Only later did I realise that this was a common thing for people with mental illness. Once they are stabilised with medication, they decide against taking it, and relapse. It wasn't long before I was listening to the voices once more.

Nowadays I accept that the taking of medications is necessary for my well-being, and gladly take them.

seven
Reflections

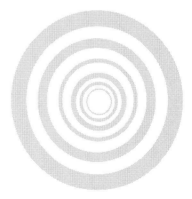

IT CAN HAPPEN TO ANYONE

Many famous people – Joan of Arc, Michelangelo, Leonardo da Vinci, Beethoven and Mozart, to name a few – suffered from mental illness. It can affect anyone, whatever their class, race, creed or social status.

Around 3 in 100 people suffer from a psychosis at some point, and about 1 per cent suffer schizophrenia. Most of these psychotic people are between the ages of 15 and 25. Around 37000 Australians are diagnosed with schizophrenia annually, and those who have a schizophrenic parent have a 10 per cent greater chance of developing symptoms. This means there are in Australia literally thousands of young people who are actively psychotic – stripped back in the prime of their lives. These are people with brothers, sisters, mums, dads and friends, all struggling to understand what the affected person is going through. The affected person may or may not realise they are sick and I have sometimes thought that if I had had a book like this one, it might have speeded up the diagnosis and recovery process. If my book does this for only a couple of people, it will have been worthwhile.

I was diagnosed with paranoid schizophrenia when I was 19. I'm now 51, a wife and a mother, a full-time secretary at school. I did not always do so well. I was diagnosed in college, lost a lot of weight, did not bathe, paced my room, thought I was going to hell, became quickly catatonic. I was in hospital for three months and put on Mellaril. I did well for years. When I went off my medication with my doctor's permission, I experienced a lot of delusions and hallucinations. I went to training to be an insurance saleswoman and took off all my clothes right there in the training. I would walk all night, then when I was tired call my husband. I thought he worked for the FBI. I got messages from the TV. I would try medicines but went off them because of the horrible side effects. I was put on Serentil. It has been wonderful but I still have stiffness, sleep 10 hours a day, dry mouth, memory loss. My last episode was 10 years ago. Up until two years ago I used to get 'messages' from people's motions. I just knew to keep it to myself. I don't think I've had any delusions for two years. For mothers out there, see? There is hope for us all. Functioning is relative but we all have a chance even with schizophrenia.

HITTING ROCK BOTTOM

Every time I hear schizophrenia mentioned in the media, it is because a tragedy has happened. I think Anne Deveson hit the nail on the head when she said it isn't the psychotics who are to blame for being violent, the true crime is the 'violence of neglect' – neglect born of ignorance.

People in the grip of mental illness often have to hit rock

bottom before any action is taken. It took me months to get to a point where I knew I had to seek treatment, and more months before I penetrated the medical system to get the help I needed.

Mental illness has been dealt with humanely only for the last fifteen or twenty years. Before that, people with a mental illness were stigmatised, and some were given lobotomies (surgical removal of the frontal brain lobe) which reduced them to a near-vegetable state such that they could not speak or move without help. Earlier still, in the eighteenth and nineteenth centuries, patients would be locked in asylums in sub-human conditions: onlookers would pay a penny to walk through the asylum and watch the residents through bars.

Today we are a little more humane, but I have friends who have been locked up in psychiatric wards, where drugs were used not only to control symptoms of illness but also to control people so that they were easy to manage.

The great tragedy of psychosis is that (by definition) it precludes awareness that something is going wrong – which means it's vital for others to show insight. I often wonder how much suffering could be prevented if the general public's awareness of mental illness was greater.

SUICIDE AND SCHIZOPHRENIA

Voices used to tell me to kill myself sometimes, and the thought of suicide crossed my mind at some of my lowest moments (bizarrely, I was convinced the conspiracy was trying to keep me alive so they could persecute me more); but I didn't seriously consider it. Many do. Suicide takes 10 per cent of people with schizophrenia. Half the people who committed suicide in Victoria in 2001 had been diagnosed with some kind of mental illness. It is a real danger – and such a waste of human potential. We can't afford to wait until a person hits rock bottom before getting help.

DUAL DIAGNOSES AND HOMELESSNESS

Another problem apparent in the mental health system is the overlap between mental illness and drug problems. They often go hand-in-hand, for ill people will 'self-medicate', turning to drugs to explain their odd feelings, or escape the chaos in their minds. The age at which many people start experimenting with drugs, the teens or early twenties, is also the age most mental illnesses manifest. Mental health systems are reluctant to deal with drug-dependent people; likewise, drug and alcohol services shy away from obvious psychotics.

I have read of movements that do not support the use of drugs to treat mental illness. Yet we know now for sure that mental illness is due to chemical imbalances in the brain, and science has proved that medication is the most effective way to secure recovery.

Drugs go with homelessness; it's also true that a high proportion of the homeless are mentally ill. Add in a high rate of unemployment and lack of activities for youth, and you have a potential flashpoint. I think this needs to be addressed.

SAFETY NET

I said before that we need greater general awareness of mental illness, so we can catch it early. Good support networks are also critical. After reading my story you may have realised that if I hadn't had loving parents and supportive friends – plus that incorruptible sliver of faith that things would work out – I too might have looked to drugs as an alternative to the anxiety and stress preying on me.

Of course, friends can't do much if you don't tell them

what's going on. Apart from the occasional 'reality check', I didn't confide much in my friends or my parents, partly because I didn't really believe I was sick. My psychosis developed so gradually and affected my reason to such a degree that I didn't see it, and I didn't know anyone else who had suffered similar delusions. Once I realised, and was open about it, I came across plenty of examples: neighbours, relatives, friends, friends of friends. If such things had been talked about more openly, I might not have felt so alone, and I might have recognised symptoms in myself.

SELF-DIAGNOSIS IN AN IDEAL WORLD

In an ideal world, with a more educated general public and less stigma attached (and I believe we making progress in this direction), anyone who develops symptoms will see health professionals at an early point in their illness, before damage is done. In an ideal world, psychotic people might research the condition themselves, book themselves in and say, 'I've been reading up on schizophrenia and I think I may have symptoms.' If this happened, they might not get to the stage of thinking everyone else is in a conspiracy, and only a low dose of medication would be necessary. (We know mental illnesses are degenerative, and this is especially true of schizophrenia: the longer it's left untreated, the less the chance of a full recovery.) The illness would not have the chance to go full-blown and cause dramas for everybody . . . in an ideal world.

ONE ILLNESS, MANY FORMS

Psychosis is not like a physical illness, which is similar for everyone. The letters and messages scattered through the book show very clearly that while there are some common denominators, there are many manifestations. I hear voices, accusing, conspiratorial. Someone else might hear music, or voices they attribute to Satan. A Native American might believe the local witchdoctor has stolen his spirit. Someone in New York thinks Oprah Winfrey can read his or her mind. It is important to understand the unique expression of mental illness for each person.

DEPRESSION AND ART

A psychiatrist once said to me that there is a connection between depression and creativity. This proposition had particular relevance to me and I brought it up in conversation with my doctor. I was always drawing and making computer art and I felt I was more in touch with my creative side on lower doses of medication. I believed that I needed to be on the edge, that if I wanted to be an artist I needed to have those tortured lows.

I debated this with the doctor and found out that someone with manic-depressive (bi-polar) disorder can actually show heightened creativity; but schizophrenia is very different, in that the psychotic person may see in an artwork wonderful ideas and themes that are unavailable to any other viewer.

Nowadays I can see that a lot of the creative work I did was plain nuts. Now I would rather be on top of the world and draw flowers than delve into the world of madness for inspiration.

Most of the images in this book were created in hindsight as a kind of art therapy, a process of defining and solidifying myself by manifesting hallucinations and letting them go; grappling with them and setting them free.

MADNESS AND MYSTICISM

Synchronistic events still abound, however. Here's a recent example. I had a book of Jungian spirituality lying around, and finally I picked it up to look at it. The page opened on 'synchronicity', a subject I'd had a great interest in earlier. When the page opened, I noticed the kettle a few metres away boiling of its own accord. What did I do? Made a coffee and read the chapter, of course.

I think a lot of people are familiar with this type of meaningful event – a chance meeting with an old friend or a premonition or 'future echo' as I call it, whereby a feeling or memory will only make sense once you have experienced something later on. These kinds of charged experiences seem to happen all the time when you are psychotic. I feel I'm missing out on the mystery of life sometimes when I disregard things as mere delusions. There's a grey area between a true mystical experience and one due to mental illness. Even before I became ill, I used to have experiences of a clairvoyant nature.

An example I can remember was going to the house of a friend from university, whose father was a world-famous portrait painter. As I went to get my bag, I said to my friend that there used to be no power point at a particular place, and that there used to be a wall with people behind it over my shoulder. God knows why I even said this; however, her father entered the hall and my friend asked me to repeat what I had said. Her father confirmed that yes, there used to be a wall there years before, behind which were servants' quarters.

Nevertheless, I think there is a romanticised notion about madness and mysticism. These extrasensory powers, if that's what they are, need to be handled carefully. Trusting your intuition can take you into dangerous territory if my experience is any guide.

Oh, and do you believe in the sixth sense? My friend has it, and she saw a white feathery floating thing passing at the back of our professor. She said it went to the window's side in front. She told this thing to me only after our school day, but she asked me if I was seeing it too, but I kept looking at the part where she is seeing it. I knew I was because I have a creepy feeling on that corner. This proves that whenever I feel something supernatural around, I am really experiencing it, I am not having delusions, whatsoever. I often hear howling and whispering noises. My sixth sense I believe is more of the auditory, although things are starting to materialise. The other night, my violin case looked as if it was blowing, getting bigger, taking a life of its own and below it, my bass guitar looked like a coffin. I could not even look at it. I did not even bother to move under covers. It was really bothering my nanny, so I went to sleep in my parents' bedroom, up to the next day, I saw the silhouette of a black cassock or thin muslin-like thing. It was really scary, it had no head. I used to think I was crazy, but now I know I am not, and that I actually see and hear these things.

A KIND OF CLOSURE

I needed to write this book. If I had my way, of course, all this would never have happened. However, I hoped that by writing about it I might be able to seal off all the chaos I had experienced; seal it up with sealing wax, put it in a cupboard or throw it to the sea. It hasn't worked out quite so simply. To this day, although my illness is at a manageable level, I am residually delusional and sometimes read odd meanings into things.

Years ago I thought people could read my innermost

thoughts. In a weird twist, now I've bared them all in black and white – a bit like psychosis but this time for real.

I am open about my experience because I believe in honesty as a path to the truth. This book is my truth and I look forward to closing it off in a last paragraph. Then, the only reminder of my deluded past will come when I pop two pills out of a friendly-looking box of Zyprexa and make an occasional visit for prescriptions to a psychiatrist who still calls me Robert.

On the plus side, had I not gone through the illness, I might have been a lot more naive in various respects. Talking to a friend who also has schizophrenia, I decided it was a beneficial experience in many respects. We have learnt humility, are open to a lot more ideas, and have a respect for reason. We also know how lucky we are to live in the age of medication. Our psychoses have revealed parts of us we might never otherwise have integrated. Given that it's past tense, I'm almost glad to have had such a powerful experience, even though I would never wish it on anyone. Playing with what cards we've been dealt has taught us a great deal. I suppose victory is that much sweeter when you have grappled with something.

HOW IS THE BOOK COMING ALONG?

When this book was nearly finished, I toyed with the idea of not publishing it. It has exposed many secrets and weaknesses, and reminded me of many things I would rather not remember – landscapes of chaos and angst. I've had to face up to a lot of truths and take responsibility for who I am. I'm no saint; like most people, I'll munch on McDonald's while I watch a World Vision advertisement.

It was tempting to forget all about it – just take my pills and get on with life. I spoke to a friend in a chat room online. He had some terrible news: his ex-partner, who was schizophrenic, had committed suicide. I offered solace to him, as he vented his confusion, anger and sadness. Then he asked how my book was coming along. I decided then and there to go ahead with it.

THE PRESENT

Nowadays, I say that I am recovered, not cured. I have a job as a graphic designer and illustrator, I have a band in which I do vocals and guitar, I have my friends and my family. I pay my taxes and do the dishes; I'm independent. I have achieved a sense of normality and live with the knowledge that a couple of pills a day will keep me slightly lethargic yet 'sane' at the same time. I can live with that.

 I am 14 years old and my older brother had paranoid schizophrenia. He committed suicide at 20 years old. The thing I want to write about is that no one thought he had it. My mom and sister knew because they started reading about it. He had all the signs of it. We live on the Navajo Reservation in Arizona. We tried to get help but the doctors and everyone thought he was just a troubled kid. It just hurts to think that they didn't want to help my brother.

Well at least I knew he had it. We knew for sure when he started acting odd. He started locking himself in his room. He wouldn't go places with us and wouldn't talk to us. He started saying that my mom was putting stuff in his food. So he didn't eat any of the food the family had made. He thought that the elders from the church we go to were after him. He even told the family that we were trying to get rid of him. When I came home from school sometimes he would sit in front of the TV and talk to it, as if the people on it were talking to him. He used to get mad when the phone rang. When his friends came over he wouldn't want to see them. Once he took off with our truck and he had no shoes or food. Nothing. We looked everywhere for him. He didn't come back until the next day. He acted as though nothing happened. He started trying to fight my other two brothers and my dad too. On his last week this happened like every night. Then one day it got so bad we had to call the police and we told them to take him to the hospital but they took him to the police station. The next couple of days we tried to get help from the doctors then again they didn't want to help us. They gave him some medication finally and then that night he was happy. The next morning was the worst day of the life I have lived. I went to school and got sent home to find that he had killed himself. My two brothers found him. It was too late. No one would help and they acted like it didn't matter. My brother was gone. Not to ever come back again. Today I miss him a lot. I have to remind myself that he isn't coming back. I think to myself that maybe he is just at school and he will come back. Sometimes I catch myself looking for him in big crowds. I want people to take mental illness serious. People out there need to know that mental illnesses exist.

We'll all miss you very much, Tony. I love you always. Your little sister.

Resources

In the case of emergencies, it is often best to look up in your local White Pages the services that are available in your area, as phone numbers often change. You can also call 12455 anywhere from Australia and ask the operator to give you the telephone numbers for mental health emergency and support services in your area.

It may also be helpful to simply go to:

www.whitepages.com

You will need to select business/government services for your search.

The 'bible' for schizophrenics is E. Fuller Torrey, *Surviving Schizophrenia, a manual for families, consumers and providers*, 3rd edn, HarperCollins, New York, 1983.

If you would like further information on schizophrenia and mental illness, the Web is a great resource. Australian and New Zealand people can go to:

www.webwombat.com.au

which searches Australian and New Zealand sites or use the list below.

AUSTRALIA

Mental Health Association NSW Australia Inc.
www.mentalhealth.asn.au

Mental Health Foundation of Australia (Victoria)
www.mentalhealthvic.org.au

Mental Health Research Institute of Victoria
www.mhri.edu.au/index.html

Mental Health Australia Online
www.mental-health.com.au

Mental Health and Wellbeing
www.mentalhealth.gov.au/index.htm

Mental Health Foundation (ACT)
www.mhf.org.au

Victorian Mental Health Service
www.health.vic.gov.au/mentalhealth/publications/index.htm

Schizophrenia Fellowship of Victoria, Inc.
www.sfv.org.au

Schizophrenia and Young People
www.health.nsw.gov.au

Schizophrenia Register
www.nisad.org.au/schizophreniaRegister/

Schizophrenia Fellowship of South Queensland Inc.
www.sfsq.org.au

Examples of support services you may wish to look up:

SANE Australia (formerly Schizophrenia Australia)
www.sane.org/
Association for Relatives and Friends of the Mentally Ill
(ARAFMI)
Schizophrenia Fellowship
Panic and Anxiety Disorders Foundation (PANX)

Other sites you may wish to research include:

Australian Institute for Family Studies
www.aifs.org.au/

Reachout
http://reachout.asn.au

SAVE
http://www.save.org

World Federation for Mental Health
www.wfmh.com

Internet Mental Health
www.mentalhealth.com

Kids Helpline
www.kidshelpline.com.au

Here are some sites dealing specifically with depression.

www.narsad.org

This is a site that caters for schizophrenia and depression, and this is helpful because the two often go hand in hand.

www.depression.org
www.depressionalliance.org
www.depression-screening.org
www.wingofmadness.com
www.dbsalliance.org

NEW ZEALAND

Mental Health Commission Homepage
www.mhc.govt.nz

Mental Health Foundation of New Zealand
www.mentalhealth.org.nz/default.asp

New Zealand Consumer Health Information
www.everybody.co.nz

Schizophrenia Fellowship of NZ
www.sfnat.org.nz